The Aleutian Kayak

KU-059-524

The Aleutian Kayak

Origins, Construction, and Use of the Traditional Seagoing Baidarka

Wolfgang Brinck

Ragged Mountain Press
Camden, Maine

Published by Ragged Mountain Press

10 9 8 7 6 5 4 3

Copyright © 1995 Ragged Mountain Press, a division of McGraw-Hill, Inc.

All rights reserved. The publisher takes no responsibility for the use of any of the
materials or methods described in this book, nor for the products thereof.
The name "Ragged Mountain Press" and the Ragged Mountain Press logo
are trademarks of McGraw-Hill, Inc.

Printed in the United States of America.

Library of Congress Cataloging-in-Publication Data
Brinck, Wolfgang.
　　　　　*The Aleutian kayak : origins, construction, and use of the
traditional seagoing baidarka / Wolfgang Brinck.*
　　　　　　　p.　　cm.
　　　Includes bibliographical references (p. 168) and index.
　　　ISBN 0-07-007893-9 (alk. paper)
　　　　　　　1. *Baidarkas—Design and construction.　　2. Aleuts—Boats.*
3. *Indians of North America—Alaska—Boats.　　I. Title*
VM357.B75　　1995
623.8290—dc20　　　　　　　　　　　　　　　　　　　　　94-43165
　　　　　　　　　　　　　　　　　　　　　　　　　　　　　　CIP

Questions regarding the content of this book should be addressed to:

Ragged Mountain Press
P.O. Box 220
Camden, ME 04843

Questions regarding the ordering of this book should be addressed to:

McGraw-Hill
Customer Service Department
P.O. Box 547
Blacklick, OH 43004
Retail Customers: 1-800-822-8158
Bookstores: 1-800-722-4726

The Aleutian Kayak is printed on recycled paper containing a minimum of 50% total
recycled paper with 10% postconsumer de-inked fiber.

Printed by Quebecor Printing, Fairfield, PA
Design and Production by Dan Kirchoff
Edited by James R. Babb, Tom McCarthy, John Vigor

To the people who built the original baidarkas.

Contents

Foreword

Nature failed to provide [the Aleuts] with the material necessary for boats, that is, wood; but on the other hand, as if in compensation, she gave them greater ingenuity for the perfection of a special new kind of fleet: the baidarka.

—Ivan Veniaminov, 1840

"The pieces of wreckage washed up first appeared in the area of Kadiak at the end of May and the beginning of June of the following year, 1800, in which months I returned from Sitkha after spending the winter there," wrote Alexander Baranov to Hieromonk Gedeon (May 28, 1807) after the *Phoenix*, the first three-masted vessel to be built by Russian colonists in North America, was wrecked off the Alaskan coast, with the loss of Archbishop Iosaf and 87 other souls. "Ship's planks were washed ashore, together with spars, the bowsprit, and the windlass; on Tugidak there appeared barrels with oil, and on Shuiak and Ukamok and in various other places even as far afield as Unalashka there appeared wax candles and several beams, flagons mixed with brine which were found by partovshchiks off Cape St. Elias. On the island of Siuklia in Chugatsk Bay two leather bindings from large books were discovered and several medium and small-sized wax candles, as many of which we received we gave to the local church here. In the Autumn of the same year, 1800, the rudder of the said vessel was discovered near Sitkha, and further into the bay beyond Rumiantsov Island two masts from the same vessel at about 56° North. We do not know of any more wreckage and there is no reliable news of the site of the wreck."

❋ ❋ ❋ ❋

Scattered over a 1,500-mile arc of rugged coastline, how were these fragments of evidence detected amidst a landscape whose convolutions have swallowed much larger vessels without a trace? Baranov's intelligence was provided by legions of keenly observant Aleut and Koniag sea otter hunters, who, two turns of the century ago, were scouring the Alaska coastline on behalf of the Russian American Company in fleets of up to 800 skin boats. Escorted by support vessels rarely larger than the *Phoenix*'s 79 feet on deck, sea otter hunting fleets ranged as far afield as Baja California and Northern Japan, with permanent detachments stationed in Southeast Alaska, Northern California, the Pribilof and Commander Islands, and the Kuriles. The Aleutian kayak, now known by its Russian name *baidarka*, was extended to unprecedented lengths, beam, and geographic range.

Few human beings have lived as amphibious an existence as the Aleuts. In what Kurt Lasswitz described (in 1901) as "The Universal Library," later portrayed by Jorge Luis Borges as "The Library of Babel" and revisited by Kevin Kelly (1994) as "The Library of Form," all possible books, all possible creatures, and, by inference, all possible kayaks, exist somewhere on the shelf. In this multidimensional space of infinite possibilities, it is the business of Evolution to search things out, discovering—or rediscovering—those combinations, however improbable, that work. As Loren Eiseley wrote (concerning life on other planets) in 1953, "it is as though nature had all possible, all unlikely worlds to make." In the Library of Kayak Form, the Aleuts opened up an entire wing. The demands of open-water sea-mammal hunting led to a cycle of physical and intellectual development that, in the words of anthropologist William S. Laughlin, allowed the Aleuts "to shuffle a whole lot faster through the [evolutionary] deck."

Circumstantial evidence suggests the development of the Aleut kayak may go back 9,000 years or more, this being the length of time, without interruptions, that human beings—sea mammal hunters, and presumably kayak builders—have been living on the shores of Umnak Island's Nikolski Bay. Bill Ermeloff and a few dozen neighbors still live here, settled tenaciously among the eastern pillars of what was once the Bering Land Bridge.

The traditions of Aleut kayak building are not extinct, but they survive, like the outlying villages (or a kayak skeleton at sea) by the strength of some very thin threads.

Bill Ermeloff remembers paddling a one-hatch baidarka that now appears, its lines reconstructed by John Heath and Eugene Arima, in the pages of this book. "Is that your single hatch there?" asked Bill Laughlin, pointing to a photograph of the kayak he had acquired from Steve Bezezekoff, on behalf of the Oregon State Museum, some 41 years ago. "Yes, that's the one!" Memories flooded back. "We used to go out between the reef and that little island there . . . we used to go out there when the rollers were coming in and then come in on the waves. . . . It was a lot of fun! You could surf all the way in!" We explained how Eugene Arima's survey would lead, eventually, to new offspring of Nikolski's last baidarka taking form. "Send up some pictures," asked Bill Ermeloff, "when you do get it built."

Wolfgang Brinck, and his fellow skin-boat builders around the world, are bringing the baidarka back to life, and none too soon. Most of us are not Aleuts—although a local revival is now under way, led by staff and students at both Kodiak and Unalaska schools. We have adopted the word *baidarka* from the Russian, with all its rich associations, in the same way the Russians adopted the craft itself from the Aleuts. The baidarka has survived intact across oceans, cultural boundaries, and time. Those who choose to build these craft today, whether for six weeks or for a lifetime, join in a collective journey whose beginnings as an interglacial experiment remain as mysterious as the origins of human intelligence itself. We are no more, and no less, than custodians of the baidarka at this moment of its journey into the 9,000 years and more that lie ahead.

GEORGE B. DYSON

Acknowledgments

I would like to thank:

Lake Michigan for tolerating my presence on its waters and not claiming my body when my ignorance would have warranted it; the trees and the willows that have contributed their wood to the frames of my baidarkas; the United States Coast Guard, the Milwaukee Fire Department, and the Milwaukee Police, all of whom have come out on more than one occasion to check on my well-being on the water; my family and friends for letting me neglect them while I worked on this book; Mike Devecka for introducing me to the idea that it is possible to build your own boat; my brother Gunnar, who supplied me with strength-of-wood data; the people at Ragged Mountain Press, especially James R. Babb, my initial contact, Dan Kirchoff, who laid out the book, and Tom McCarthy, the editor who took it from manuscript to finished product; John Heath, George Dyson, and John Brand for taking the time to look at my book and offer comments and encouragement. I would also like to express my gratitude to them for researching and documenting traditional skin boats and passing their knowledge on to the rest of us.

I would also like to thank my friends and fellow paddlers, Mike Giunta, Bob Boucher, and Martin Honel for reading the manuscript and offering comments.

Introduction

1

There is pretty good evidence that the type of kayak you're about to build was made in the Arctic for at least 2,000 years. The Aleuts who built these boats called them *ikyax*; the Russians who colonized Alaska called them *baidarkas*. It also appears that skin boats of some kind have been used by Aleuts for 9,000 years or more.

Kayaks and umiaks, made of wood and skin, don't survive for long, but the stone and ivory parts of hunting gear used with these boats do. Since the hunting gear used with kayaks and umiaks differs, it's possible to deduce the age of these boats from remnants of their associated gear.

Baidarkas were used as hunting craft in the Aleutian Islands just as kayaks were in the rest of the Arctic. Before the Russians arrived, baidarkas coexisted with the large open *baidaras*—the Aleutian version of the umiak. Umiaks were used to haul gear and make family migrations from the winter villages to the summer hunting and fishing grounds. The Russians confiscated and destroyed most of the baidaras to prevent the Aleuts from escaping their enslavement. The Russians did, however, promote building baidarkas since the boats were essential to the sea otter hunt, the prime reason for the Russian presence.

While the design of the baidarka precedes the Russian presence in the Aleutians, the Russians no doubt influenced baidarka construction by providing the Aleuts with steel tools.

Figure 1-1. A model of an early kayak from Ekven, East Siberia. It's about 2,000 years old and resembles a decked-over umiak.

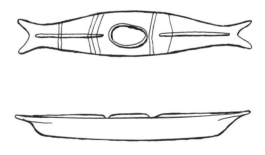

Steel tools no doubt made the building of baidarkas easier. According to George Dyson, author of *Baidarka*, the Russians also homogenized the baidarka's design by forcing large hunting parties to undertake extended voyages in search of sea otter pelts, thus bringing together builders from previously isolated islands.

The first drawings and written accounts of baidarkas were made after Vitus Bering's "discovery" of Alaska in 1741.

Though baidarka specimens now in museums were collected mostly between the mid-19th and mid-20th centuries, many of the drawings and accounts produced during the one hundred previous years of European contact show and tell of boats that are in many ways different from the museum specimens. Most notably, the drawings show much shorter boats than are in museums.

Did the Aleuts actually built shorter boats, or were the artists who drew them and the writers who described them simply inaccurate observers? I don't know, but I'm inclined to think that those early observers were careless, perhaps biased by their knowledge of small European boats, which were much beamier for their length.

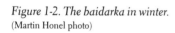
Figure 1-2. The baidarka in winter.
(Martin Honel photo)

In any case, the design of the baidarka we're concerned with here is based on museum specimens from the early part of

this century. I think these are sound designs and a much better example to follow than questionable descriptions recorded by 18th-century explorers.

Why Build a Kayak?

The only way to know what it feels like to paddle a skin-on-frame kayak is to build one and paddle it. You can't very well go to a museum and check one out. There are people who will build you a custom skin-on-frame boat, but I think a good part of the appreciation of a skin boat comes from having built one yourself.

If you're going to spend 80 to 100 hours building one, you might want to feel that your skin boat is in some way superior to a plastic boat you can buy in a store. I feel no personal need to justify building skin boats. The pleasure of building and paddling my own boats is justification enough. I do feel that skin-on-frame boats are superior to plastic boats in some tangible ways. When you build your own boats, you'll have your own reasons for believing that skin boats are better, but for starters, here's my list. Use it, if you want, to defend skin boats—or your decision to build one.

Skin boats have more spirit than plastic boats. Objects reflect their creator's spirit, which you impart to your boat as you work on it. The longer you work, the more of your spirit the boat will have. Plastic boats have very little spirit because the whole point of manufacturing is to keep costs down by minimizing human effort. At best, plastic boats will have very little spirit. At worst, they'll have a negative spirit, which comes from the boredom and hostility often found in factories. I'm not saying that you can't improve a plastic boat's spirit. As you paddle it, its spirit will develop, but I don't think a plastic boat will ever match a handmade wooden boat in spirit no matter how much time you spend with it.

The history of the parts that make up your boat contributes to its spirit just as your attitude does when you build it. The materials comprising your boat are all so simple that with a little research, you can find out where each of them came from. If you are sensitive to how much violence you need to do to others and the environment before you get out on the water to paddle, making your own boat and controlling the source of the materials is the perfect method. For instance, you can make many of your boat parts from recycled lumber, assuring yourself that you're not a party to cutting down any new trees, even if the lumber you are using may originally have come from an old-growth stand.

The deck beams of my last few boats have all come from lumber recovered from home remodeling projects. I have a friend who gets his wood for deck beams by visiting building sites and recovering lumber scraps from dumpsters. I am no purist about building materials and will use synthetics when it makes sense. I do think, though, that my boats have a stronger spirit if I can feel that all the materials were collected and assembled in the proper manner.

While the essence of mass production is that one size fits all, you can tailor a skin boat to fit your own body and discover the pleasure of having something uniquely your own—a pleasure normally reserved for the wealthy in the form of a tailored suit or handmade shoes. If you are of average build, fit may not be a big issue because it is for you that manufacturers make boats. If you're very small or very large, however, a boat that fits may not be within your reach unless you make your own.

You can tailor a skin boat to your temperament and to the temperament of the waters that you paddle. Your first boat may be something of a shot in the dark, but as you take it out and use it, you will think of ways to improve it. Maybe you'll want to make it larger to carry more gear. Maybe you will want to make it lighter or shorter or longer or with a bigger cockpit or with a flatter bottom or with more V. You might want to paint it to blend in with your paddling grounds, or bright orange so the Coast Guard can see you better.

You can "tune" a skin boat, and if you build more than one, the quality of your boats will improve. You will become sensitive to the properties of the materials you use, and to the tension of the skin and the lashings and the flex of the wood, and you'll learn to balance these for optimum effect. Plastic boats are not tunable. They come in one stiffness for fiberglass (stiff) and another stiffness for polyethylene (limp).

If you're short on money but long on time, you can build a skin boat for a fraction of the cost of a plastic boat. I don't think that the cost of plastic boats is prohibitive for someone who really wants to paddle, but when you think of all the other things $2,000 can buy, the idea of building your own boat may become even more attractive.

Why Build an Aleutian Kayak?

I have built both Greenland and Aleutian kayaks, and I feel the Aleutian kayak is a better cruising boat because it has more space for gear. It has more parts than a Greenland kayak so it takes a little longer to build, but the shape of the hull is simpler and it is a little easier for the first-time builder to get right.

How Strong is It?

Skin-on-frame boats are quite strong. I would rate them somewhere between fiberglass boats and polyethylene boats. I was once picked up by a wave and surfed into a big rock that brought me to a dead stop. Based on the force of the impact, I expected to be picking splinters out of my thighs, but to my surprise the boat was not damaged. A skin-on-frame boat responds to force much the same way that a tree does. It bends out of the way and returns to its resting position when the force is removed. Of course, a baidarka is not indestructible. If you should exit your boat in the surf and have it fill with water, it will weigh several hundred pounds. And, if crashed into a rock, the force of this weight might crack some ribs. But even if your boat has cracked ribs and stringers you can paddle it, since the skin and the lashing are still holding the broken parts in place.

Another common concern seems to be the skin's strength. People worry that a sharp stick or rock might poke a hole in it. I have yet to see a sharp stick where I paddle, and I avoid sharp rocks, usually a concern only when landing and launching. In either case, a canvas skin will at most lose some paint where a fiberglass boat will get a deep gouge or cracked gelcoat. When I have to make an emergency surf landing on a rocky beach, I much prefer skin to fiberglass.

Canvas does have its limits and will get punctured or torn. If you desire a skin that is stronger than the frame of your boat or if you expect your boat to take a lot of abuse, look into using synthetic materials.

Building Experience

You don't need woodworking experience to build a baidarka successfully. If you can learn to use a handsaw, a block plane, and a drill, you can build a baidarka. (I haven't included detailed instructions on using and maintaining hand tools, but there are plenty of good books on the subject in public libraries.)

In any case, you will learn as you build, and a good deal of the teaching will be done by your tools and materials. As you get a sense of what your tools can do and how your materials respond, the building process becomes simpler and more pleasurable.

Paddling Experience

I assume that if you build a kayak you will also want to paddle it. If you have never done any kayaking before, be warned that you may need a little practice before you feel comfortable in this boat.

Most U.S.-made sea kayaks have beams of anywhere from 23 to 26 inches and relatively flat bottoms. Contrast this with the 21-inch beam and relatively deep V-bottom of the Aleutian kayak that you will build. I think that the wide beam and flat bottom of commercial boats has to do with the economic reality that people will not buy kayaks that they cannot paddle without practice.

If you plan to paddle your kayak only in protected waters, are building it mostly for the pleasure of building, and don't expect to paddle it more than a few times each season, by all means make it wider. You'll have a boat you can use and feel comfortable in. It's better to have a boat that deviates from the Aleutian norm if you use it than a faithful replica that gathers dust in your garage because you don't feel comfortable with it.

Building Time

If you have never built a boat before, give yourself about four months to finish this one. Building the baidarka's frame takes about two months of spare time, and sewing the cover and painting it takes another few weeks or so. The first skin boat I built took me almost six months from start to finish, the result of having a manual that was pretty sketchy about a lot of the construction details.

I've attempted to write *The Aleutian Kayak* to allow you to build step by step, without losing a lot of time on experimentation and trial and error. If you have never built a boat or worked on a long-term project before, persistence will be your most important asset. It is easy to hit a roadblock and want to give up. If you have any friends even marginally interested in boatbuilding or woodworking, you might want to take one of them on as a building partner. With a partner to give you moral support, you're much less likely to quit if you encounter a problem.

What It Costs

You can buy all the materials needed to make the boat for under $200 in 1995 U.S. dollars. If you decide to build another boat, you can build that one for under $100. The cost of materials breaks down roughly as follows:

Lumber, $30

Paint, linseed oil, and turpentine, $40

Canvas (wholesale), $35

Canvas (retail), $70

Thread, lashing twine, rope, and needles, $20

This all adds up to a maximum of $160 if you have to pay the retail price for canvas. If you want to keep your costs under $200, you have another $39.99 to spend on tools or to cover the increasing cost of lumber.

The Steps of the Process

There are a number of different ways to make a baidarka, depending on the materials available, the kind of tools you have, and so on. Rather than try to deal with different construction methods at the same time, I have chosen to present a single way of building the boat. This makes the presentation of the building process a lot more straightforward. Alternative construction methods are discussed in appendices.

What to Do When Things Go Wrong

I won't categorically say that something will go wrong when you build a boat. I've made it through whole boats without any problems. On the other hand, building a boat has so many steps that there is a good chance you will run into some problems. The most important thing when encountering one is not to get discouraged. There is no rush. When I can't immediately see a solution, I usually back off and wait a day, which gives me time to think—and I always come up with something. Talk the problem over with your partner, if you have one. But don't quit.

Appendix 1 has some troubleshooting tips. These won't necessarily cover everything that could possibly go wrong, but you will get a flavor of the general approach to dealing with problems.

Building Baidarkas Outside of the U.S.A.

All measurements in this manual are specified in English units of feet and inches since this is still the prevalent system in the U.S. For the benefit of builders outside of the U.S., metric equivalents are supplied in parentheses. Inches were converted to centimeters by multiplying by 2.54. Pounds became kilograms by dividing by 2.2.

I have divided metric conversions into three categories. In the first category, you may use the exact conversions—the actual dimensions of the boat, such as length, width, and depth —as they are.

The second category is approximate conversions, or the metric conversions of approximate English dimensions. For instance, if I suggest that you make a boathook from a stick approximately 5 feet long, you don't have to make it exactly 152.4 centimeters in length. Any stick from 140 cm to 160 cm will probably do.

The third category is conversions of cut lumber dimensions. A board may be sold in the U.S. as ¾ inch x 7½ inches (1.9 cm x 19 cm) in cross section. Your lumberyard may not have any boards this exact size. If this is the case, get the closest possible equivalent.

Finally, I would like to point out a peculiarity of the U.S. lumber trade that may be confusing to builders outside the U.S. Lumber is described by its size before it was planed, even when it is not sold in an unplaned condition. So 1 x 2s are really ¾ inch thick and 1½ inches wide. The 2 x 4s universally used for construction are really 1½ inches thick and 3½ inches wide.

I have tried to avoid confusion by giving *finished dimensions* of lumber in all cases. However, if you see any references to 1 x 2s or 2 x 4s, you'll know what I'm talking about.

2 The Nature of the Boat

To get some idea of the kind of boat you're about to build you should understand the Aleutian kayak's properties and behavior.

The Parts of the Boat

Figure 2-1. Replica of an Aleutian baidarka from Atka, originally surveyed by David and John Heath.

The names of the kayak parts shown below are keyed to Figure 2-1, though I'm not sure there are any standard English names for

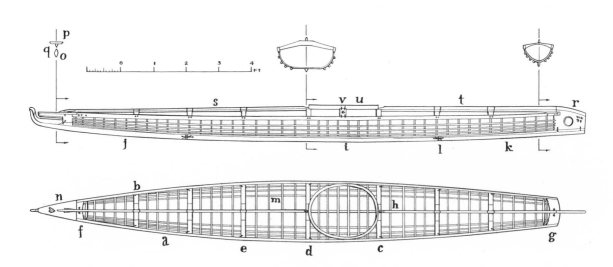

most parts. Where possible, I have used traditional boating terms. Where traditional terms don't apply, I have improvised.

Aleutian terms for parts of the boat have been recorded by Knut Bergsland; see *Contributions to Kayak Studies* for details.

a. gunwales

b. deck beam

c. backrest

d. knee brace

e. foot brace

f. bow crosspiece

g. tail crosspiece

h. rib

i. keelson, center section

j. keelson, bow section

k. keelson, tail section

l. keelson joint

m. hull stringer

n. bow

o. lower bow

p. upper bow piece

q. bow slit

r. tailfin

s. front deck stringer

t. rear deck stringer

u. cockpit coaming

v. coaming stanchion

The Origin of the Boat

The boat you'll build is an Aleutian kayak used by hunters in the latter part of the 19th century and the early part of the 20th

Figure 2-2. Baidarka replica covered with canvas skin.

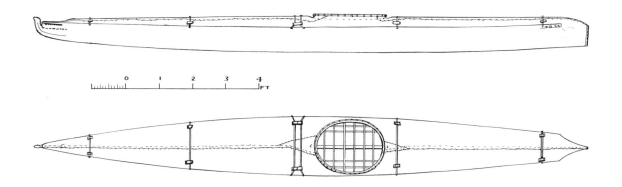

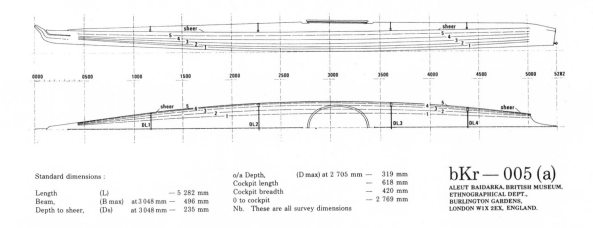

Standard dimensions :

Length	(L)		— 5 282 mm
Beam,	(B max)	at 3 048 mm —	496 mm
Depth to sheer,	(Ds)	at 3 048 mm —	235 mm

o/a Depth,	(D max) at 2 705 mm —	319 mm
Cockpit length	—	618 mm
Cockpit breadth	—	420 mm
0 to cockpit	—	2 769 mm
Nb. These are all survey dimensions		

bKr — 005 (a)
ALEUT BAIDARKA, BRITISH MUSEUM,
ETHNOGRAPHICAL DEPT.,
BURLINGTON GARDENS,
LONDON W1X 2EX, ENGLAND.

Figure 2-3. An Aleutian baidarka in the British Museum. Courtesy of John Brand.

century. The boat in Figure 2-1 is a replica of a boat in the Hearst Museum (formerly the Robert H. Lowie Museum) in Berkeley, California. It was collected in Atka by Margaret Lantis in 1934. Figure 2-2 shows the same replica boat with its skin on. The boat in Figure 2-3 is in the British Museum in London. No information on its origins is available. Note that even though these boats come from different islands, their shape and dimensions are remarkably similar. George Dyson attributes this similarity to the homogenizing effect of the Russian presence in the Aleutians.

The Baidarka Changes with Time

A kayak made of natural materials changes over time, settling and adjusting itself in the first six months, especially if used frequently. The canvas skin will tighten and put pressure on the ribs. Ribs that stick up a little higher than others will be pushed forward or backward, eventually leveling with their neighbors. In time, all the ribs will flatten somewhat. You'll notice that the boat's shape changes slightly and subtly. Its keel might drift off to one side or the other for a while, but eventually it seems to straighten itself again. The paint will wear, the nose may droop a little, the cockpit coaming will elongate, and so on.

Keeping all this in mind, realize that the drawings on the following pages show somewhat idealized versions of real boats. Your boat will look pretty much like the boats in the drawings but with the lumps, bumps, and irregularities that result from using natural materials.

Form and Function

If you are tempted to tinker with the design of the baidarka presented here, I'll give you a list of what I feel are key baidarka design features and their functions. If you decide to modify any of them, you will at least have some idea of how it will affect the boat. If you are interested in a detailed technical treatment of this topic, read George Dyson's paper, "Form and Function of the Baidarka: The Framework of Design," which appears in *Contributions to Kayak Studies*.

The Aleutian kayak was designed to be paddled on the ocean around the Aleutian Islands that separate the North Pacific from the Bering Sea. The winds and the currents there are some of the most severe in the world. Not only did the Aleutians have to be very good paddlers to survive under these rough conditions, they also had to have a boat design that was tuned to these conditions. It seems to me that the design they evolved over the centuries is not likely to be improved upon. Any gross modifications to the design are likely to give you a boat of lesser seaworthiness.

Elements of Seaworthiness

After having read much about the seaworthiness of aboriginal kayaks, I built one and took it out paddling on Lake Michigan on a windy late-March day. After a short time paddling, I capsized and spent the next 15 minutes swimming the boat back to shore. So much for seaworthiness.

Luckily, I was wearing my drysuit. As I carried my boat back to the car, firefighters with grappling poles approached from land as a Coast Guard boat approached from the water. Someone had seen me swimming. After that incident, I spent the next year practicing my roll every time I went out on the water and eventually got good enough that I didn't have to swim my boat any more.

The moral of the story is that the seaworthiness of a kayak has as much to do with the skill and experience of the paddler as it does with the boat itself. No matter how good you or your kayak are, there will always be weather that can get the better of you. Humility and respect are the proper attitudes when you put your boat in the water. When you paddle in rough water, you soon realize that the key to survival is cooperation and grace, not domination. You need to know your limits and those of your boat, and you need to get off the water or stay off the water when you get close to those limits.

Potential Paddling Speed

George Dyson has promoted the idea that Aleuts were capable of paddling their kayaks at 10 miles an hour (16 km/h). There are historical accounts that they did. However, don't be disappointed when your kayak doesn't go that fast. Speed in a kayak is a lot like seaworthiness—it depends as much on the paddler as on the boat. For one thing, studies of Aleut skeletal remains have shown that the bones in their arms were quite a bit bigger in diameter than those of contemporary Russians or other peoples of today. The implication is that the heavier bones supported quite a bit more muscle. The norm for Aleutian paddlers may well have been strength and stamina found only in Olympic-class paddlers today.

The normal cruising speed for a kayak with a 16-foot (488 cm) waterline length is about 4 miles per hour (6.4 km/h). People in races of some distance have averaged 9 miles per hour (14.4 km/h). Paddling all day against a headwind with a heavily loaded boat, I have averaged as little as 2 miles per hour (3.2 km/h).

While the speed of a kayak depends a lot on the paddler, as a builder you can control certain aspects of the boat that affect speed: skin friction and tightness, flexibility of the frame, and width and weight of the boat. A rough or bumpy paint finish causes more skin friction than smooth paint does. An Aleutian kayak's frame is intrinsically flexible because of the light weight of the frame members. However, loose lashings or loose skin will cause a kayak to paddle as badly as a rubber raft. Tight lashings and tight skin are essential to good performance.

If you increase the length, width, or weight of the boat, you also increase the amount of surface area in contact with the water, which in turn increases resistance to forward motion. Increased weight also causes you to expend more energy accelerating the boat—and since it decelerates between strokes, that's every time you apply power.

The Importance of Volume

Volume is the total amount of space enclosed by your boat, and it must be enough to keep paddler and cargo afloat. In the case of an Aleut, this was probably 160 pounds (73 kg) for the paddler and another 75 pounds (38 kg) for gear and sea otter pelts or ballast stones. The volume should be sufficient to give the boat 3 to 4 inches (7.5 cm to 10 cm) of freeboard or clearance between the waterline and the sheerline.

Less freeboard means that water will wash across the deck more often. More freeboard means that more of the boat will be affected by wind pressure. An inch (2.5 cm) of freeboard can make the difference between making progress in a strong wind and standing still.

Since Aleuts went on long trips and had to haul their gear and pelts in their boats, they probably built their boats with enough volume to handle well when loaded. This meant that the boats probably sat a little high in the water when empty.

The width, length, and depth of the kayak all relate to volume. Increasing any one dimension will increase the boat's volume. If your weight is under 180 pounds (82 kg) and you want to make the boat wider to give it more stability, you might also try making it shorter to keep the overall volume from going up.

Another aspect of volume is affected by the part of the hull that sits in the water. If you make a high-volume boat you'll have more of the bottom and less of the sides in the water. If you make a low-volume boat you'll have comparably more of the sides in the water. Two boats with roughly the same hull shape will behave quite differently if one sits high in the water and the other sits low.

Width and Stability

If you have never paddled a kayak before or if you have only paddled one of the wider recreational kayaks with a beam of 23 inches (58 cm) or greater, you might find an Aleutian kayak with a 21-inch (53 cm) beam a little tippy. The easiest way to make your kayak more stable is to make it wider. The question is, should you? My answer is no; at least not without good reason. There are some good reasons why you may want to make your kayak wider, and we'll come to them later, but let's begin with a few reasons why you should not.

This may not make sense at first, but a narrow kayak with a deep V-bottom is more seaworthy in rough water than a wider, flat-bottomed kayak. I first had this explained to me in a seminar given by Frank Goodman, the designer of the Nordkapp kayak. With a 21-inch (53 cm) beam, the Nordkapp often is accused of being tippy, and so requires its designer to have a ready defense.

What makes a wide, flat-bottomed kayak stable in flat water is the tendency of the bottom of the boat to stay parallel to the water's surface. A narrow, V-bottomed boat would just as soon lean over, and so is perceived as being tippy. A narrow boat needs the agility of its paddler to keep it upright. In rough water, the flat-bottomed boat still tends to stay parallel to the surface of the water, only now the surface of the water is tilting and the paddler needs to lean to one side or the other to keep the boat from capsizing. The flat bottom also makes the kayak susceptible to sliding sideways, especially in breaking waves.

In rough water, the narrow boat needs to be kept upright by its paddler just as it does in flat water, so rough water doesn't cause any new anxiety for the paddler. The rough water does not tilt the narrow boat to one side or the other, so the paddler does not have to lean to stay upright, but simply paddles and keeps his or her body vertical.

H. C. Petersen in his book, *The Skinboats of Greenland*, tells of a special storm kayak that hunters there once built, which was narrower and had a deeper V-bottom than the normal fair-weather kayak. This boat was so unstable without a paddler that it would tip to one side if you laid a paddle on the deck off center. There are stories of similarly unstable Aleutian kayaks, supposedly built before the coming of the Russians.

One windy day, I stood by the shore of Lake Michigan and watched a large Canada goose and a small diving duck swimming in the breaking waves. The Canada goose with its large buoyant body surfed and slid a few feet sideways every time a wave broke. The small diving duck, which sat a lot lower in the water, was not moved around by the breaking waves at all. The waves simply washed over it and it kept right on swimming without any loss of ground. Kayaks that are good in storms are like the diving duck.

Having given you reasons why a narrow kayak is better in stormy water, let me now give you some reasons why you might want to build a wider, more stable boat. After you spend all that time building a boat, you should feel comfortable in it. While most people can learn to paddle a narrow boat, some will never feel comfortable in one. If you are one of these people, make the boat wider. Some otherwise very athletic people have bad balance and need a wider boat. And ultimately, all kayaks are unstable and need a paddler to keep them upright. Don't build a narrow boat just because you think it is more sporting. Build a boat you can feel comfortable in. Incidentally, women and children do better than men in narrow boats because they seem to have a lower center of gravity.

If you have never been in a kayak before and are wondering whether a 21-inch (53 cm) boat is too narrow for you, go to a kayak symposium or to a boat dealer who lets you take boats out on the water, and try a narrow boat. If you feel comfortable with that width or think you could learn to feel comfortable with it, go ahead and make your boat 21 inches (53 cm) wide. If you aren't comfortable, make your boat wider. An inch or two makes quite a difference. Avoid making the boat wider than 23 inches (58 cm) unless your hips necessitate it, because you will pay with reduced performance.

Of course, if your primary concern for the boat is not sportiness but carrying capacity, or you aren't concerned much about speed or never intend to go near any rough water, by all means make the boat as wide as you need.

Length

The length of the Hearst Museum boat is 16 feet 9 inches (510.5 cm). The length of the Oregon State Museum boat is 17 feet 1 inch (521 cm). Both of these boats are roughly 20½ inches (51.9 cm) wide. There isn't any point in making the boat any longer unless you want to turn it into a cargo barge.

I made one replica of the boat in the Hearst Museum, which ended up at 18 feet 6 inches (564 cm) since I didn't want to shorten the lumber I used for the gunwales. A 17-foot (518 cm) version of the same boat is noticeably more responsive and has a livelier feel because the shorter boat pivots more quickly when going over waves. The longer boat has more inertia. It starts climbing a wave earlier, but it also waits longer to pivot over the top of the wave—and when it finally does, it slams down on the other side like a breaching whale.

The Effect of Depth

Depth from the top of the gunwales to the bottom of the keelson is about 8½ inches (21.9 cm). Don't make the boat any deeper unless your knees won't fit under the knee brace. Unless you are quite heavy or carry a lot of gear, greater depth to the boat translates into more boat sticking out of the water and more surface area for the wind to use as a sail.

The more a boat protrudes from the water, the higher its center of gravity and the less stable it becomes. A taller boat is harder to paddle because the higher deck forces you to lift your paddle higher.

Cockpit Position

The cockpit in an Aleutian kayak is positioned more than halfway back so that there is more boat in front of the paddler than behind. It may seem that the boat is not balanced correctly, but

Figure 2-4. When the baidarka is afloat its deck ridge and sheerline are more or less parallel to the surface of the water.
(Martin Honel photo)

it is. When the boat is sitting in the water, the deck ridge, which is almost straight, is pretty much parallel to the water. When viewed from the side, a baidarka looks a lot like a floating log. The extra length of the boat in front of the paddler makes it rise to a wave sooner and keeps the paddler dry.

The Effect of a V-Bottom

The cross section of the boat in the vicinity of the keelson is V-shaped. The V helps the boat maintain a straight course. It also makes it harder to turn, but on open water the ability to turn quickly is rarely required.

The amount of V in the vicinity of the cockpit is somewhere between 10 and 15 degrees upward from the horizontal. The amount of V decreases if you make the boat wider and increases if you make the boat narrower. If you are making the boat narrower than 21 inches (53 cm) because you are building it for a smaller person, you might also want to decrease the depth of the keelson to keep the amount of V from becoming excessive.

Figure 2-5. The pronounced V-bottom of the baidarka gives it a better grip on the water than flat-bottomed commercial kayaks.

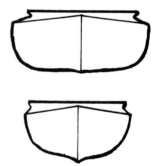

Why a Ridged Deck?

In moderately rough, breaking waves, water slides off on either side of the center deck ridge, which is preferable to water washing along the deck and slamming you in the chest. But if the waves break hard enough, you get slammed in the chest anyway.

Drawback of the Internal Frame

One of the few drawbacks of skin-on-frame boats is that the frame takes up space inside. This means that a plastic boat of a size comparable to your baidarka will have greater storage capacity. If you take excursions with people who have plastic kayaks, you may feel a bit guilty about not carrying as much stuff. If it really bothers you, you can stick with other skin-on-frame paddlers as companions.

The Strength of Your Boat

The Aleuts covered their boats with animal skins, which lasted a year, maybe two, before they had to be replaced. This means that the Aleuts had frequent access to all parts of the frame. This allowed them to build boats as lightly as possible since repair and replacement of cracked or broken ribs and stringers was not a problem.

A canvas skin, on the other hand, lasts at least five years and if treated carefully, can last for 10. This increases the chances that you'll crack a rib or stringer or otherwise damage some part of the frame long before the skin needs replacing. If you want to make a repair, you'll need to remove the skin, repair the part, and replace the skin.

A cracked rib or stringer is not a big deal on an Aleutian boat, which has 40 ribs and eight hull stringers. A break here and there will not incapacitate your boat. However, if you do much rough kayaking, these breaks will accumulate and you'll have to slit the seams on the boat long before the skin is worn out. If you want to save yourself some maintenance and don't mind the extra weight, make the ribs and stringers heavier and stronger.

Parting Comments

The design of a boat is inevitably a compromise between conflicting requirements such as stability and speed, or strength and light weight. I found that my first boat took a long time to build because I spent more time agonizing over various design decisions than building. The building process will be a lot easier if you can accept the idea of not making a perfect boat the first time out. Build the best boat you can, then take it out and paddle it for six months. Without a doubt you'll think of ways to make your next boat better. Go to kayaking symposiums and meet other builders. Trade construction tips and stories. Paddle as many other boats as you can, and learn.

Fitting the Boat

3

The Aleutian kayak featured in this manual should fit people up to 6 feet (183 cm) tall and 180 pounds (82 kg) in weight. If you are bigger, or substantially smaller, you might want to change the boat's dimensions.

Traditional Dimensions

Traditional kayak builders recorded the dimensions of their boats in terms of armspans, handspans, length of forearm, width of thumb, and so on. One such set of measurements has come down to us from Bill Tcheripanoff by way of Joelle Robert-Lamblin. The set of measurements she recorded was for a two-hole kayak. She also translated these measurements into centimeters, which makes it possible to take the dimensions of a one-hole kayak and translate them into body-based dimensions. The results of this translation are shown in Figure 3-1.

If you are thinking of using your own body as a yardstick

Figure 3-1. The traditional way to size an Aleutian baidarka, according to Bill Tcheripanoff. Armspan is 64 inches (161.9 cm). Elbow to fingertips is 17 inches (43 cm). Handspan, thumb to middle finger, is 8 inches (20 cm). Thumb to knuckle of middle finger is 5½ inches (14 cm).

for building your boat, here are a few words of warning. First, if your armspan exceeds 64 inches (163 cm), you will get a boat longer than 17 feet (5.18 m). I have built longer boats but find that I prefer the 17-foot (5.18 m) length. If your armspan is less than 64 inches (163 cm), you can probably use the body dimensions described above.

Second, boatbuilders settle on boat dimensions after much trial and error. This means you should first build a boat according to the recommendations of this book. Then if you like the way it handles, record the dimensions of the boat in terms of your body dimensions.

Third, a good boatbuilder will not build a boat strictly to one set of dimensions. If you build a boat for someone else you need to fit the boat to that person. If you build a boat for yourself, you will vary the basic dimensions to make a fast boat or a stable boat or a strong boat or a light boat. In other words, a set of dimensions is only a starting point.

Intended Use

If you intend to use your kayak on open water, in wind and waves, your best bet is to make it just large enough to fit you. Excess size will work against you when you have to fight difficult conditions. If you plan to use your kayak mostly on rivers or small inland lakes, you can afford to make it wider or with a bigger cockpit without too much loss in performance.

Interior Height

The space between the ribs and the deck beams forward of the cockpit must be large enough to accommodate your legs. The space in the vicinity of the foot brace must be large enough to accommodate your feet and footgear. These measurements are more critical if you paddle in cold climates, since you also have to allow for several layers of clothing.

The Ideal Width

The Aleutian kayak is at its widest at the knee brace. The suggested width in this manual is 21 inches (53 cm). The width of

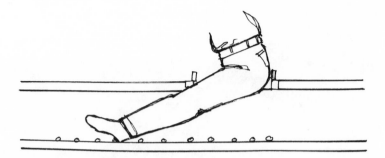

Figure 3-3. The cockpit must be long enough so your rear end clears the back of the cockpit coaming when your knees are up against the knee brace.

the cockpit is 18 inches (46 cm). If your hips are wider than 17 inches (43 cm), add an inch of width to the boat for each additional inch of width of your hips. You should also make the cockpit at least an inch wider than your hips.

If you make your boat wider without making it deeper, it will be more stable on flat water but more difficult to roll. If you've never paddled a kayak before and are more interested in flat-water stability than rough-water performance, adding an inch to the width won't do much harm, but it makes quite a difference in feel.

Cockpit Length

The cockpit must be large enough for you to enter and exit without too much difficulty. If the cockpit is too short, you won't be able to get into the boat. If it is too long, breaking waves are more likely to punch through the sprayskirt and fill your boat with water.

Figure 3-4. To measure the length of your lower body, sit against a wall or door and measure from the wall to the balls of your feet.

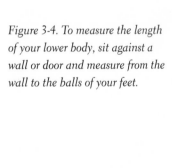

I suggest a cockpit length of 24 inches (61 cm)—long enough for people whose length from the bottom of their feet to the small of their back when sitting is less than 48 inches (121.9 cm). To measure this distance, sit on the floor with your back against a wall and your paddling shoes on your feet. Measure the distance from the wall to the balls of your feet. Increase the length of the cockpit by the amount your measurement exceeds 48 inches (121.9 cm). If your measurement is close to 48 inches (122 cm) and you have stiff knees or your kneecaps stick out, add 2 inches (5 cm) to the length of your cockpit.

If you'll paddle mostly in protected waters, make the cockpit opening longer for easy entry without having to worry about breaking waves punching through your sprayskirt.

Length of the Boat

Your size really has no bearing on how long the boat should be. Just remember that if you make your boat longer, you'll need bigger arms to paddle it. An overly large boat is not a pleasure to paddle. Stick with the basic 17-foot (518 cm) length unless you feel the need to carry a lot of gear.

4 Tools and Materials

Traditional kayaks were made with a few simple tools. Modern reproductions of traditional kayaks can be made the same way. Here is all you'll need to build a kayak.

Tools You'll Need

Not all these tools are essential—some are just handy and make the job go faster.

Figure 4-1. Power drill (top) and hand drill (bottom). The power drill can be used one-handed, leaving the other hand free to hold the material.

Hand Crosscut Saw

Get an eight-point saw (seven teeth per inch), 26 inches (66 cm) long. This is a good saw for cutting lumber to size. More teeth in a saw give you a finer cut but also make for slower cutting.

Dovetail Saw

This is a small saw with fine teeth, used for sawing the ends of deck beams to tight tolerances, and for trimming dowels and cutting tenons.

Drill and Bits

Use any kind of drill you like as long as it accepts the following sized bits. Drill-bit size for dowels should be 1/64 inch (0.5 mm) smaller than the dowel to ensure a tight fit:

⅜ inch (10 mm) for round rib mortises

¼ inch (6 mm) for lashing holes

¹¹⁄₆₄ inch for ³⁄₁₆-inch dowels

¹⁵⁄₆₄ inch for ¼-inch dowels

Block Plane

The block plane is a small plane that you can use one-handed while you hold the work with the other hand. I use one with the blade set

Figure 4-2. A collection of small planes, all of which can be used one-handed. The Japanese plane in the center is pulled, the other two planes are pushed.

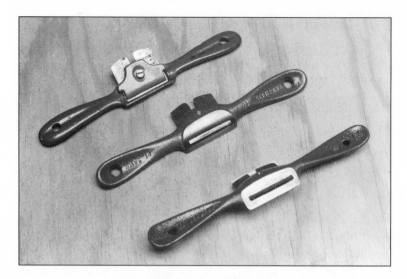

Figure 4-3. Top view and bottom view of some spokeshaves. The middle spokeshave has a rounded sole, making it suitable for shaving inside curves. The bottom spokeshave has a flat sole.

at a 20-degree angle. I saw one recently at Sears for $15. You can pay up to $50 for one of these planes, but that isn't necessary.

Spokeshave

You'll need this tool for rounding the corners of your chine stringers and for shaping ribs. Spokeshaves come with both flat and rounded bottoms. I use one with a rounded bottom.

Hammer

You'll need a hammer to drive dowels. You'll also use it to drive in nails during deck setup and to pull them out afterward. If you have to buy a hammer, get a fairly small one. A heavy carpenter's hammer is more likely to do harm than good.

Crooked Knife

This is my all-round utility knife, capable of carving flat, convex, and concave parts. It's like a one-handed drawknife, and I prefer it to a straight-bladed knife for shaping parts. The crooked knife has always been part of the aboriginal tool set: Kayak builders would split their wood from logs, shape it with an adze, then finish it with a crooked knife. In North America, carvers used beaver incisors for the blades of their crooked knives before they had access to steel.

If you're right-handed, hold the knife with your palm up and the blade pointing to the left. To carve, pull it toward you. In

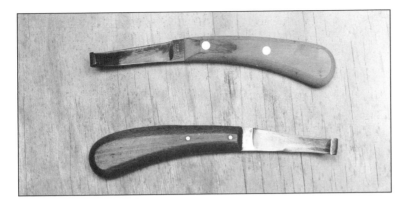

Figure 4-4. Left-handed crooked knife (top) and right-handed crooked knife (bottom). You pull these knives toward you like a drawknife.

days gone by, farmers used these knives to trim horses' hooves, so you can get them at antique fairs or order them from places that specialize in unusual hand tools.

Straight Knife

You can get by without a crooked knife if you have a straight one, but it must have a fixed blade and a handle that won't give you blisters when you use it.

Adze

The adze is like an axe shaped to carve wood rather than split it. The one I have has a flat blade on one side and a scoop on the other, and it's one of the best tools I've acquired. With a little practice, you can work to within 1/16 inch (1.5 mm) of a line, then use your crooked knife or plane to do the final finishing. The adze is a little slower than a bandsaw in cutting irregular-shaped pieces such as deck beams, but it's a lot more portable and about $400 cheaper.

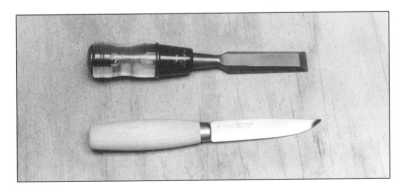

Figure 4-5. A chisel (top) and sloyd knife (bottom). The curved part of the knife blade lets you carve concave shapes.

Figure 4-6. Combination adze/axe (top) and small carving adze (bottom). The adze is useful for removing excess wood quickly.

If need be, you can do some rough trimming with a small axe, but the heads on axes are considerably heavier and will fatigue your arm much more quickly.

Clamps

Clamps of all sizes and types are handy to have but not essential. You can trial-lash with string or temporarily assemble things with nails if need be. Still, if you have clamps, you'll use them. For

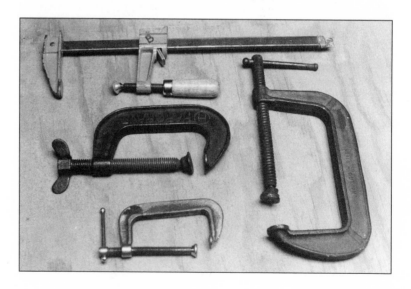

Figure 4-7. You can never have too many clamps. I use the smaller ones the most often.

clamping ¾-inch (1.9 cm) lumber, 3-inch (7.6 cm) C-clamps are a good size. For larger pieces, use 4-inch (10 cm) clamps.

Wood Chisel

A sharp ¾-inch wood chisel is handy for trimming wood off the end of a deck beam if, for instance, you're within $\frac{1}{32}$ inch (1 mm) of your final length. It's also a good tool for cleaning up mortises and tenons. I have found the ¾-inch (1.9 cm) width to be a good all-round size.

Sewing Needles

You'll need both a straight and a curved canvas needle, both of which are available from boating supply houses. Variety stores may have repair kits with a canvas needle and some small curved needles, which will save you a mail order.

Electric Saw

An electric saw, whether table saw, circular saw, or radial arm saw, will speed up the process of ripping long pieces out of a plank. Electric saws are dangerous tools. If you have never used them, get a demonstration and a safety lesson from someone who has.

Marking Gauge

A marking gauge is a fast way to run a line down the length of a

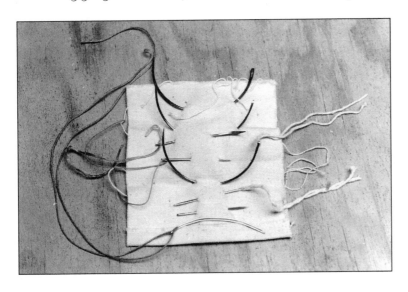

Figure 4-8. An assortment of straight and curved needles. The bottommost needle is a doubled piece of wire used to thread twine through lashing holes.

Figure 4-9. A marking gauge. The single pin (bottom) is used for such tasks as marking centerlines. The double pin (top) is used for marking mortises.

board at a fixed distance from the edge. You can do the same thing with a pencil, though.

Square

A square is handy for drawing lines at right angles to the edge of a board, but if you trust your eye, you can get by without it.

Sliding Bevel

A sliding bevel lets you mark a line at a fixed angle and also lets you check the angle of your gunwales. For this boat you can get by with simply cutting the end of a short length of wood of ¾ inch (1.9 cm) by 1½ inch (3.8 cm) cross section at the right angle and using that for both marking and checking bevels.

Figure 4-10. A square (top) and sliding bevel (bottom). Both tools are used to mark wood accurately. If you have a good eye, you can probably do without them.

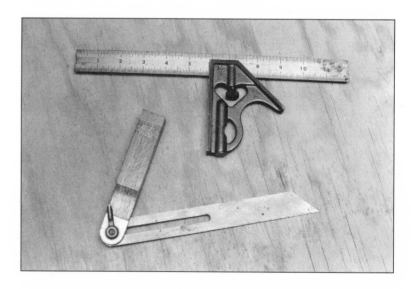

Sawhorses and Workbenches

A pair of sawhorses is all the bench you'll need. The sawhorses will support the frame of the boat, with space left over to support parts while you're working on them. A sturdy bench about knee high is also handy. At knee height, either your knee or a foot can clamp down on a piece of wood while you're working on it, with no time lost to clamping and reclamping.

Sharpening Hand Tools

You may need to sharpen your knives, chisels, and planes in the course of building the boat. Many tools, especially knives, do not have a usable edge when you buy them and require sharpening prior to use. There are whole books devoted exclusively to sharpening hand tools. If you intend to sharpen your own tools and have never done so before, read one of these books or have someone experienced show you how. Many people turn good tools into bad tools by assuming they know how to sharpen them. Don't be one of these people.

If your handsaw is sharp when you start building the boat, it will still be sharp when you are done. It is possible to sharpen your own saw, but it is generally more convenient to take it to a hardware store to have it done.

Work Space

You'll need a work space 20 feet (610 cm) long and 8 feet (244 cm) wide. Wherever your space is, make sure you can get your boat out of it when you're done. I currently build my boats in my basement and get them out through a basement window. This limits me to boats no more than 30 inches (76 cm) wide and 14 inches (36 cm) high. For a kayak, there's plenty of room to spare.

Materials

With the exception of the skin, the baidarka can be made from materials readily available at local hardware stores and lumberyards—lumber for the frame, string for lashing, twine for sewing the skin, and linseed oil and paint for sealing the frame and the skin.

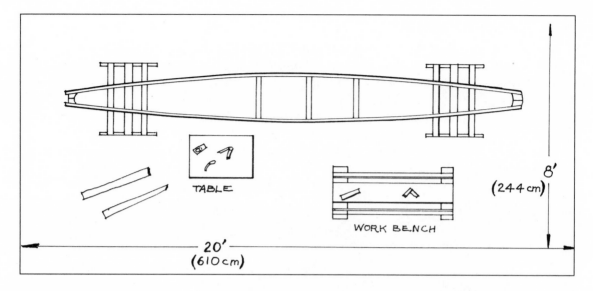

Figure 4-11. Minimum work space requirements. More space is better because it lets you step back and spot irregularities in the shape of your boat.

An Overview of Lumber Requirements

Ideally, you can get all your boat lumber in a single trip to the lumberyard. To help you with your shopping, I have laid out a list of materials in pictorial form.

Selecting the Lumber

Your boat's wood should be knot-free, which means buying clear lumber, though a knotted piece with sufficient length between the knots can be cut up for some of the shorter pieces, such as deck beams.

The boat-part dimensions in this book assume soft wood of some sort. According to Joelle Robert-Lamblin, Aleuts preferred spruce for most of the frame and yellow cedar for the ribs. Yellow cedar, after soaking in water for several days, could be bent cold with some help from the builder's teeth. Aleuts also had access to red cedar but didn't use it because they preferred the greater strength of spruce.

Unless you want to order lumber from a specialty marine lumber dealer, you will have to make do with the lumber available in your area. Building-grade spruce with knots in it is readily available in my area, but clear spruce is not. With some judicious cutting, I can get knot-free pieces long enough for deck beams.

For the gunwales, I use what clear lumber I can get—Eastern white pine, yellow pine, and red cedar—none of which is as good as spruce. Yellow pine is heavy, and white pine and red cedar are soft and more prone to damage than spruce. However, you can compensate for lesser strength by making the gunwales a little deeper.

When you buy your lumber for the gunwales and the other long pieces, find wood with the straightest grain. Avoid pieces with the grain running at an angle to the long faces of the board.

Deck stringers and keelson parts can be cut from 8-foot lengths. Chine stringers are best cut from 16-foot (488 cm) pieces but can be made from shorter lengths scarfed together. (See Chapter 5 on basic techniques for details on how to make scarfs.) Gunwales should also be cut from 16-foot lumber.

If you buy two ¾-inch x 7½-inch x 16-foot (1.9 cm x 19 cm x 488 cm) pieces of knot-free lumber, you will have enough for the gunwales, the stringers, the deck stringers, and the keelson.

Figure 4-12. Your lumber requirements at a glance. It may look like a lot of wood but it amounts to no more than about one plank in the average suburban deck.

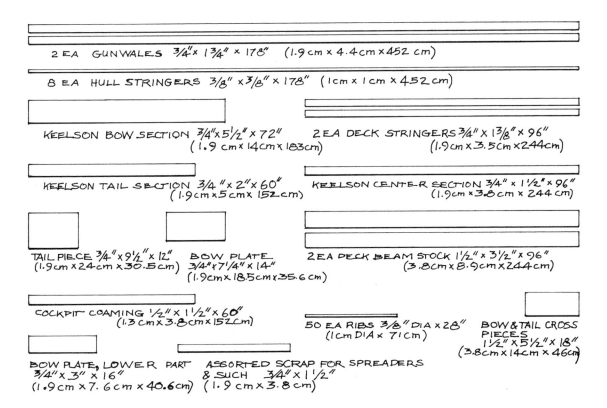

2 EA GUNWALES ¾"x 1¾" x 178"   (1.9 cm x 4.4 cm x 452 cm)

8 EA HULL STRINGERS ⅜" x ⅜" x 178" (1 cm x 1 cm x 452 cm)

KEELSON BOW SECTION ¾"x5½" x 72"   2 EA DECK STRINGERS ¾" x 1⅜" x 96"
       (1.9 cm x 14 cm x 183 cm)   (1.9 cm x 3.5 cm x 244 cm)

KEELSON TAIL SECTION ¾ " x 2" x 60"   KEELSON CENTER SECTION ¾" x 1½" x 96"
       (1.9 cm x 5 cm x 152 cm)   (1.9 cm x 3.8 cm x 244 cm)

TAIL PIECE ¾"x 9½" x 12"   BOW PLATE   2 EA DECK BEAM STOCK 1½" x 3½" x 96"
(1.9 cm x 24 cm x 30.5 cm) ¾"x7¼"x 14"   (3.8 cm x 8.9 cm x 244 cm)
                    (1.9 cm x 18.5 cm x 35.6 cm)

COCKPIT COAMING ½"x 1½" x 60"
       (1.3 cm x 3.8 cm x 152 cm)   50 EA RIBS ⅜" DIA x 28"   BOW & TAIL CROSS
                                           (1 cm DIA x 71 cm)   PIECES
                                                                1½" x 5½" x 18"
                                                          (3.8 cm x 14 cm x 46 cm)

BOW PLATE, LOWER PART   ASSORTED SCRAP FOR SPREADERS
¾" x 3" x 16"   & SUCH ¾" x 1½"
(1.9 cm x 7.6 cm x 40.6 cm) (1.9 cm x 3.8 cm)

Two 1½-inch x 3½-inch x 8-foot (3.8 cm x 8.9 cm x 244 cm) pieces of spruce or fir are sufficient to make the deck beams. Some knots are all right if they are spaced at least 20 inches (51 cm) apart on the average.

A 2-foot (61 cm) long, 1½-inch x 5½-inch (3.8 cm x 14 cm) piece of construction-grade lumber should be sufficient to make the bow and stern crosspieces.

Some Wood Numbers

The following numbers will give you some basis for comparison when you select wood for your boat. The numbers come from the *Wood Handbook*, which is put out by the Forest Products Laboratory in Madison, Wisconsin. The properties of wood vary

Strength and Weight of Some Common Woods

Wood Type	Specific Gravity	Modulus of Elasticity
Western red cedar	0.31	0.94
	0.32	1.11
Eastern white pine	0.34	0.99
	0.35	1.24
Sitka spruce	0.37	1.23
	0.40	1.57
Longleaf pine	0.54	1.59
	0.59	1.98
White ash	0.55	1.44
	0.60	1.74
Red oak	0.56	1.35
	0.63	1.82
White oak	0.60	1.25
	0.68	1.78

with its moisture content, so two sets of numbers are given—a low range for green wood and a high range for dry wood. These numbers are intended for rough comparison only. Additional factors such as brittleness, tendency to split, spacing of annular rings, and so on all affect the properties of wood. Most important for long pieces such as gunwales and keel parts is straight grain.

The first number is the specific gravity, which is the density of a material as compared to water, which has a specific gravity of 1.0. Higher numbers mean higher weight for the same volume of wood. The frame of a baidarka made of spruce will weigh about 23 pounds (10.4 kg). A frame of the same dimensions made out of yellow pine, of which longleaf pine is an example, would weigh 23 x (.56/.38) or 38 pounds (17 kg). You can see that if you use heavier lumber, you may want to reduce the size of the frame members to keep the weight down.

The second column of numbers is the modulus of elasticity—basically the wood's stiffness. Higher numbers mean stiffer wood. The numbers can also represent the strength of the wood. So if you were to use yellow pine instead of spruce, you could probably cut back the cross-sectional area of the wood by a factor of 1.3/1.7. This means that you can cut back either the height or the width by this factor, but not both.

Rib Material

I make baidarka ribs out of two- or three-year-old willow twigs. They are supposed to be at their best when harvested in the winter months, though I've collected them at other times. In the spring or early summer, the outer layer of newly grown willows is still brittle and not firmly attached to the inner layers. If you have to do extreme bends, the outer layer tends to crack more easily than if you were using winter wood, but the problem isn't so bad that it should stop you from building in the spring or summer months. Besides, the bark peels much more easily in the spring and summer when there is more sap in the wood.

I have also made ribs out of steam-bent white ash and red oak. Traditional wooden-boat builders frown on red oak because it is prone to rotting; white oak is better. The use of rot-resistant wood in a kayak is not as critical as in traditional wooden boats since kayaks are not left to sit in the water.

Lashing Materials

Lashing string should be roughly ¹⁄₁₆ inch (1.5 mm) in diameter. You can use nylon as well as jute, hemp, or flax. Cotton isn't very strong so I would avoid it. Jute is adequately strong if it is polished. Hemp and flax are even better but hard to come by. The problem is that synthetics are cheaper and generally stronger than natural fibers, so they have displaced the natural fibers in all but low-grade package-wrapping string.

Traditional kayak builders used whatever lashing material was available and convenient. Before the advent of trading posts, they used baleen or thin strips of animal hide. Later they tended to use string.

Most of your lashing holes will be ³⁄₁₆ inch or ¹⁄₄ inch in diameter. The rule is that you keep lashing until your lashing hole is about half filled, and if your string is too fine, you need too many turns of lashing.

You might also want to get a cake of beeswax and draw the string across it until it gets nice and sticky. This makes for tighter lashings because the string doesn't slide back if you're forced to release tension while lashing.

For lashing the ribs, flat ribbon material is good because it doesn't leave a lump under the skin. Tandy Leather sells a product called artificial sinew, which is unbraided waxed nylon. Two strands of this will do the job for ribs.

Where to Get Tools and Materials

Here's a list of companies that sell hand tools and boat construction materials by mail order. All of them have catalogs, and some may charge a small fee to send them. If you live outside North America, you might want to find other sources.

Hand Tools

You should be able to get most of your hand tools from the local hardware store. If not, the places listed below can supply all your hand tool needs. All have catalogs of woodworking tools and will send them to you either free or for a few dollars. If you live outside the U.S., you are probably better off getting your tools locally.

Garret Wade Co.
161 Avenue of the Americas
New York, NY 10013-1299

Reinhold Brothers Company
2402 West Lisbon Ave.
Milwaukee, WI 53205-1499

Woodcraft
210 Wood County Industrial Park
P.O. Box 1686
Parkersburg, WV 26102-1686

If you like going to garage sales, flea markets, and antique shows, you can often pick up hand tools at good prices. At the last one I went to I picked up three crooked knives and my friend Bob picked up some hand planes.

Canvas

You might find canvas locally at awning or tent shops, but if you need to order it, try the Astrup Co., which has offices in many cities. To locate the nearest one, get in touch with their headquarters:

Astrup Co.
2937 W. 25 St.
Cleveland, OH 44113
(216) 696-2820

Needles and Twine

The businesses listed below both have needles and twine. I've always bought my twine and rope locally, but if you are interested in exotic stuff like tarred line, the Wooden Boat Shop has it.

Canvas Crafts
501 N. Fort Harrison Ave.
Clearwater, FL 34615

Canvas Crafts has both straight and curved needles and beeswax, which is handy for waxing your thread before sewing or lashing.

The Wooden Boat Shop
1007 N.E. Boat St.
Seattle, WA 98105

Kits

Boucher Kayak Co.
1907 Ludington Ave.
Wauwatosa, WI 53226

Bob Boucher sells kits with almost everything (except for the long pieces of wood) you need to build your own boat, including rib material, coaming, canvas, twine—the works.

Dyson, Baidarka & Company
435 West Holly St.
Bellingham, WA 98225
(206) 734-9226

George Dyson sells needles, lashing twine, and high-strength synthetic skin materials as well as skin coatings. He also distributes plans for baidarkas of his own design to be constructed out of aluminum tubing and synthetic skin.

Organizations

If you are looking for more information about skin boats or if you are simply looking for other skin boat makers to talk shop with, or to go paddling with, join an organization. Here are two:

Baidarka Historical Society
P.O. Box 5454
Bellingham, WA 98227

The Baidarka Historical Society devotes itself exclusively to baidarkas. It has an annual meeting and distributes baidarka-related books to its members whenever such books become available.

Native Watercraft Society
P.O. Box 26121
Wauwatosa, WI 53226

The Native Watercraft Society collects and distributes information about all kinds of native boats, including kayaks. They put out a newsletter three times a year and have an annual rendezvous.

Basic Techniques

5

Rather than interrupt the flow of the construction sequence in later chapters, I'll explain basic techniques such as pegging and lashing here. If you have prior woodworking experience, you can probably skip this chapter.

Standards of Workmanship

In most of the Arctic, the shape of wooden objects was roughed in with an adze and finished with a crooked knife, giving a characteristic hand-carved finish to items made of wood.

In our culture, power tools and glossy varnishes let woodworkers put machinelike finishes on wooden objects. As a matter of fact, a machinelike finish now seems to be the hallmark of good craftsmanship.

I feel a machine finish is inappropriate on a replica of a baidarka. I prefer the hand-carved finish of the originals. If you get a chance to look at some kayaks in museums, do so and emulate the spirit of their construction.

Marking Wood

The point of marking wood is to indicate unambiguously where you want to cut it.

You will be fitting most of the parts of your kayak to other

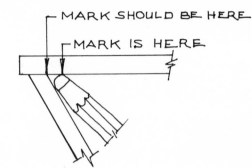

MARK SHOULD BE HERE

MARK IS HERE

parts that are already in place. If you use a pencil to mark parts, remember that the pencil line has thickness. To minimize inaccuracy, keep your pencil sharp and make your mark as close to the edge as you can. The drawing at left shows in an exaggerated manner how lines you mark can be off from where you want them.

When marking wood for trimming to length, make an X on the part you're going to trim. This is especially important if the piece to be cut off is about the same length as the piece that you'll use. By the time you get the wood back to the bench to cut it, you're likely to forget which half was the good half and which half was the cutoff.

Cutting off Wood

A saw cut has some width to it. When you cut, cut on the side of the line you marked with the X. If you center your saw on the line, the piece will end up too short.

Many of the parts of the boat, such as the deck beams, have compound angles. Until you become more sure of your cuts, cut about ¹⁄₁₆ inch (1.5 mm) longer than you need and trim the piece to fit.

Figure 5-2. Cut on the side of the line with the X on it (top). If you cut right on the line (bottom) your piece will turn out too short.

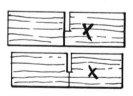

Using a Marking Gauge

The marking gauge is a handy tool for marking a line a fixed distance from an edge. Since the mark is made by a sharp steel pin, the line is generally more precise than a pencil line. Kayak building does not demand this kind of precision, and the marking gauge is not essential, but I recommend it simply because it is handy for such things as marking the centerlines on the edge of a piece of wood for a paddle, and the centerline on the bottom of the gunwales for drilling rib mortises.

Drilling Pilot Holes

If your drill wanders away from the mark, try making a small hole that your larger drill bit can follow. You can punch a small starter

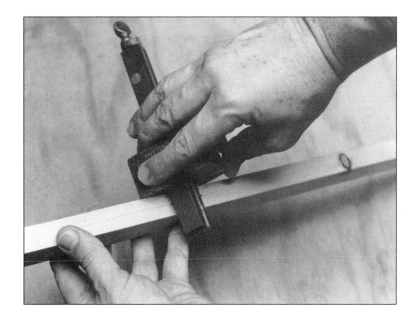

Figure 5-3. A marking gauge is a handy tool for marking centerlines.

hole with a nail or drill it with a small drill bit. The pilot hole does not have to go all the way through the piece. Pilot holes are especially important if you intend to drill wood that has hard rings or dark wood with softer, light wood in between. Without a pilot hole, the drill tends to slide off the hard wood into the softer wood.

Figure 5-4. A small pilot hole will keep your drill from wandering.

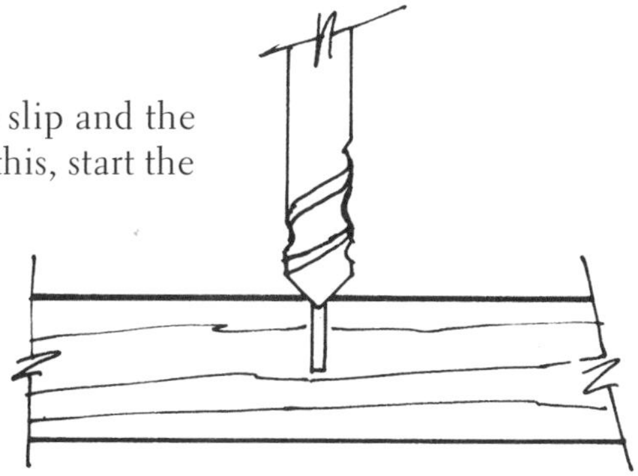

Drilling Holes at an Angle

When drilling angled holes, your bit will tend to slip and the hole will not end up where you want it. To avoid this, start the hole with the drill bit going straight into the wood, and when you have a ⅛-inch (3 mm) start or so, tilt the drill and continue the hole at the angle you want.

Drilling Through-Holes

When you drill a hole through a board, the wood on the back face tends to tear out. For the most part, this doesn't matter on a boat, but if you want to avoid this problem, back the board you are drilling with a piece of scrap wood. The back of the hole will then be as clean as the front.

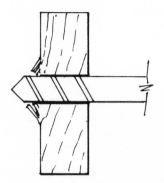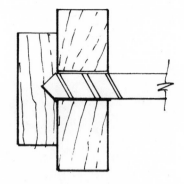

Figure 5-5. A drill coming out of the back of a piece of wood causes tear-out (left). Backing up the hole with a small piece of wood prevents this problem.

Drilling Doweling Holes

When drilling holes to dowel two boat parts together, such as a deck beam to a gunwale, immobilize the two pieces first by nailing them together temporarily. If you leave the head of the nail sticking out, you can remove the nail after you're done drilling. If you just hold one piece of wood up to the other and drill, the second piece has a tendency to slide to one side or the other when the drill goes into it.

Planing Wood

Figure 5-6. When drilling holes for dowels, temporarily immobilize the two pieces of wood with a small nail. Leave some of the head sticking out so you can withdraw it later.

Use a block plane to do final shaping of boat parts and to remove saw marks from plank edges. A block plane can be worked with one hand, leaving the other hand free to hold the piece you are working, with its end resting on a bench or sawhorse. The block plane eliminates the need to clamp your stock, which saves a lot of time.

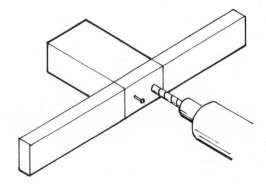

Gluing up Parts

Aleuts used glue on their hats but probably not on their boats. If you are a purist and don't want to use glue, then don't. It is not essential in the construction of the baidarka. I sometimes use it because I find it easier to glue up a large part like the upper bow piece than to carve it out of one piece. Sometimes I'll glue up wider pieces such as the tailfin because I have only narrow pieces lying around and don't want to make a special trip to the lumberyard.

If you decide to glue up parts, use a waterproof glue such as resorcinol or epoxy. Epoxy is probably a better choice since it requires less careful clamping to make a strong bond.

Pegging or Doweling Parts

Regardless of what size dowels you use, use a drill bit that is 1/64 inch (0.5 mm) smaller than your dowel. When you drill holes by hand, the drill tends to wobble and the holes will be slightly over-sized. With an undersized drill bit, you get a good tight fit on the dowels. But don't make the hole too small or you could break off the dowel when you try to pound it in, or split the piece you are trying to dowel. In general, doweled construction in the kayak does not use glue, which allows the dowel joints to do some moving under stress.

Lashing

The preferred lashing material in aboriginal times was baleen, which was elastic but did not stretch when wet. Strips of seal hide were also used, but only when baleen was not available.

Nowadays, just about anything can be used. I have used nylon string as well as jute. I prefer the feel of plant fiber over nylon. Plant fibers generally swell and so tighten up when they get wet. But they will attract mildew and rot if you leave them wet. They don't stretch as nylon does, and if you soak them with linseed oil after lashing they should be water-resistant for a long time.

When you lash two pieces edge to edge, like the keelson to the tailfin, you need to drill lashing holes, which should be 3/16 inch (4 mm) to 1/4 inch (6 mm) in diameter. Your lashing cord should be about 1/16 inch (1.5 mm) in diameter; take about six turns with the cord. To get the cord through the hole, make a needle by doubling over a 6-inch (15 cm) piece of wire.

Scarf Joints

The Hearst Museum boat has some scarfed hull stringers. My guess is that straight-grained lumber in 15-foot (457 cm) lengths

Figure 5-7. To thread your lashing string through small holes, make a lashing needle by bending over a piece of wire (top). Lashing holes should be 3/16 inch to 1/4 inch in diameter (bottom).

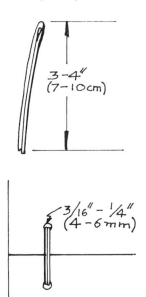

3-4"
(7-10cm)

3/16" - 1/4"
(4-6mm)

was hard to come by and was reserved for the gunwales where strength was more critical. Hull stringers aren't primary structural members and could be scarfed together from shorter pieces.

The scarfs used on the hull stringers were hook scarfs, whose stepped construction locked the two sides into each other and kept them from sliding apart. The scarf joint was held together with several turns of string lashing.

It is also possible to use glue scarfs to make long boards out of short boards. This is one way to get 15-foot (457 cm) gunwales out of 8-foot (244 cm) boards. Glue scarfs are used in traditional wooden boat construction and are apparently effective. Epoxy is recommended for glue scarfs because it doesn't have to be clamped very carefully. The planks to be scarfed need to overlap by 9 inches (23 cm) when glued face to face. The rule is that the overlap must be 12 times the thickness of the board to be effective. John Gardner in *The Dory Book* gives a very thorough treatment of glue scarfs (see References, page 168). If you intend to use glue scarfs, you will find his book very helpful.

You can also scarf planks edge to edge, which I've seen on a 19th-century Greenland boat. The main advantage of this technique is that it lets you reinforce the joint with dowels, an asset when you don't have access to a lot of clamps.

Figure 5-8. You can join sections of hull stringer by using a hook scarf. Lashing around the scarf keeps it immobilized.

Figure 5-9. Two pieces of wood can be scarfed face to face (top) or edge to edge (bottom). The edge scarf can be held together by dowels alone, while the face scarf is best glued.

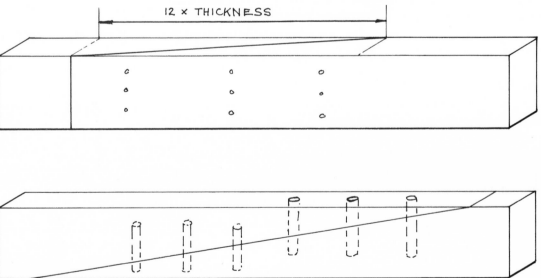

12 × THICKNESS

If you can get 16-foot (488 cm) planks, you don't need glue scarfs. I mention them on the outside chance that you can only get shorter lumber. I've used glue scarfs on some ¾-inch x 1-inch (1.9 cm x 2.5 cm) pieces where I had to cut a knot out of an otherwise clear piece of wood. Not using the piece of wood with the knot in it would have meant another trip to the lumberyard.

Keeping the Boat Aligned

The problem with a kayak is that there is hardly a right angle in the whole thing. Most of the parts are curved and come together at odd angles. There is, however, one important requirement for a boat: If you run a straight line from the middle of the bow to the middle of the tail, there must be the same amount of boat on both sides of the line.

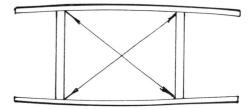

The best way to make sure your boat meets this requirement is to run a string from the bow to the stern when you are putting your deck together and make sure the gunwales stay the same distance from the string on both sides. You can also check by measuring diagonals on the spaces defined by the gunwales and the deck beams. If the deck is square, the diagonals will be equal.

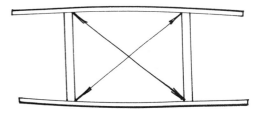

Figure 5-10. If your deck is square (top), diagonals between deck beams will be equal. If your deck is not square (bottom), diagonals will not be equal.

6 The Paddle

A paddle is a good thing to make at the beginning of your boat-building odyssey. For one thing, making a paddle gives you a chance to become familiar with your tools. For another, it gives you a completed product in a matter of days, and you'll get a feeling of accomplishment right off the bat.

Aleut builders sought to make paddles light and strong, which they did by using a lightweight wood, keeping the paddle blade thin, and putting a stiffening ridge on the back of the paddle.

Sizing the Paddle to Fit You

The paddle, like everything else on your boat, is fitted to your body. If you have any doubts about size, make the paddle a little oversized for starters. You can always trim it down later. You can also make different paddles for different conditions. A smaller paddle is like low gear on a bicycle and is effective for paddling into a headwind or with a heavy load.

To determine the length of the paddle, measure from the ground to the tip of your fingers with your arm stretched overhead. That measurement is the overall length of your paddle. But if you've made your boat wider than 21 inches (53 cm) you will need to make your paddle a little longer since you'll have farther to reach to get it into the water.

The width of the blade at its widest point should be such that it comfortably fits your hand for rolling or bracing, or 3 inches to 3¼ inches (7.6 to 8.2 cm). The width of the paddle shaft between the blades should be about 25 inches (64 cm), or shoulder width plus two hand widths. Another way to size the paddle

Figure 6-1. Your paddle should reach as high as your arm with fingers extended.
(Robert Boucher photo)

is to make the distance between your hands the same as the width of the boat forward of the cockpit. This spacing optimizes power and minimizes movement of your arms between strokes. If you make your boat wider than 21 inches (53 cm) you may also have to increase the spacing between the blades.

Choosing a Paddle Blank

You can either get a piece of wood thick enough to carve your paddle from without any gluing, or you can get some thinner pieces of wood and glue them together to obtain the right thickness. Both methods have advantages. Starting with one thick piece of wood means you have more carving to do and you waste a lot of wood, but you don't need six or eight clamps to hold the pieces together while the glue is drying.

Choice of wood depends on what is available. A wood such as spruce is probably best if you can get it because it gives you good strength with light weight. White pine and red cedar are light in weight but more likely to break unless you make the blades thicker than you would with spruce. Yellow pine is strong but heavy, so you need to reduce blade thickness to bring down the weight.

Regardless of which thickness you choose, the board you start with should be free of warp and 8 feet (244 cm) long and 3¼ inches (8.2 cm) wide.

Preparing the Paddle Blank for Carving

Before you start carving, mark centerlines on both the front and

Figure 6-2. With your hands positioned at the roots of the paddle blades, the space between them should be about the width of your shoulders. (Robert Boucher photo)

Figure 6-3. Dimensions of the paddle blank. A glued-up version is shown but you can also use a single thicker piece of wood.

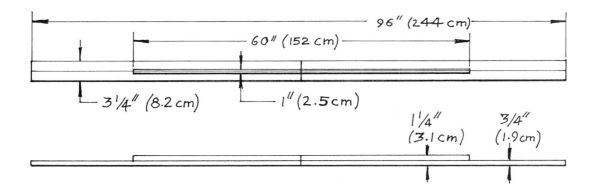

96" (244 cm)

60" (152 cm)

3¼" (8.2 cm)   1" (2.5cm)

1¼"
(3.1 cm)   3/4"
(1.9cm)

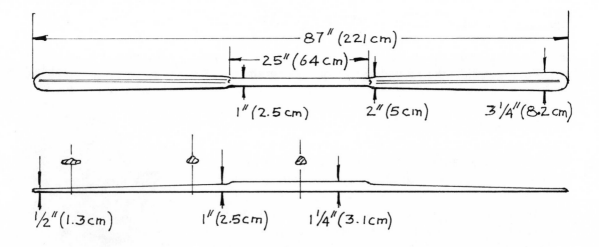

Figure 6-4. Dimensions of the finished Aleutian paddle.

back faces of the paddle blank, and the shape of the paddle on the top face of the blank.

Carving the Paddle

Start by removing wood so the paddle has the right shape when viewed face on. Power tools are fastest but not necessary; I use an adze for the rough shaping.

Once your paddle has the right shape, use a spokeshave and a plane to shape the shaft. The cross section of the shaft is like a triangle with the corners rounded off.

Using a hand plane and starting where the blade widens, taper the thickness of the blade toward the tip. Use a crooked knife or curved wood chisel to remove wood on either side of the center ridge, which runs down the length of the blade.

Finishing and Painting the Paddle

Finish plane the paddle and sand it if necessary—rough edges on the shaft quickly raise blisters. Before you do the final painting and sanding, give the paddle a try on the water to make sure it feels right. (The correct way to hold an Aleutian paddle is with the ridge on the face of the blade facing back.) Make alterations as needed.

When you are happy with the shape of the paddle, paint it red and black, the traditional Aleut colors. If you use oil paint,

dilute it sufficiently with turpentine so you do not get a glossy finish, which is slippery and dangerous, especially on the shaft.

Figure 6-5. A typical Aleutian paint scheme. The dark parts are black and the light parts are red ocher.

Alterations

If your paddle feels too cumbersome in action, cut an inch off either end and try it again. If it still feels too long, cut off some more. If it feels too heavy and you think you can lighten it without compromising its strength, take a plane to it.

A Different Paddle

Figure 6-6 shows a paddle with a slightly different pattern from the Aleut model. This one is symmetrical and closer to a Greenland model, and its main advantage for the first-time paddle carver is that the blades have only flat planes and don't require any scooping with a crooked knife. This paddle can be completed using only a plane and a spokeshave.

Figure 6-6. An alternate paddle pattern, which is a little easier to carve than the standard Aleutian pattern.

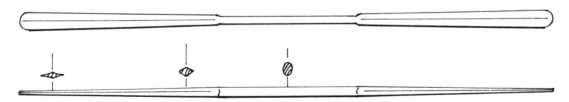

7 Building the Deck

The deck consists of the gunwales, deck stringers, and the bow and stern cross blocks. As part of its construction, you will also drill the mortises for the ribs in the bottom edge of the gunwales.

The instructions in this chapter assume that you want a 17-foot (518 cm) boat. If you want to go with a length other than 17 feet (518 cm) you will need to adjust the dimensions accordingly. Thickness dimensions for the lumber assume that you are using soft wood.

These instructions also assume that you will dowel the deck beams to the gunwales. If you want to use mortise-and-tenon construction for the deck, see Appendix 3 for details.

Cutting the Gunwales

You need two pieces of wood, each 1¾ inches (4.4 cm) wide and 14 feet 10 inches (451.9 cm) long. Thickness should be anywhere between ¾ inch (1.9 cm) and 1 inch (2.5 cm), depending on

Figure 7-1. View of the ends of three planks showing the kinds of grain you are likely to encounter when looking for gunwale stock. View 1 shows quarter or vertical grain, which is best for gunwales but hard to come by. View 2 shows a plain-sawn plank, which is your second-best choice. View 3 shows a slash-sawn plank, which should be your last choice because it is the least likely to give you two matched gunwales.

1

2

3

whether you bought planed or rough lumber. This length of gunwales together with the bowpiece and tailpiece will give you the overall length of 17 feet (518 cm) for the boat.

The gunwales must be the same size and each must have the same flexibility as the other, in both vertical and horizontal directions. If the gunwales flex differently the deck will tend to turn out lopsided. The most reliable way to get matched gunwales is to cut both from the same plank. The plank will ideally have straight grain running parallel to the edges of the board, called vertical-grain or quarter-sawn lumber.

Quarter-sawn lumber is ideal but may be hard to get. It's more likely that you'll get plain-sawn lumber, which has the grain running at different angles along the board.

If you cut your gunwales from plain-sawn lumber, use a piece at least 9½ inches (24 cm) wide, which will allow you to get enough pieces out of the plank to have at least two with matching flexibility. You can then cut up the leftover pieces for stringers.

Figure 7-3. Cut your plank as shown. The two pieces in the middle are most closely matched and will be the best candidates for gunwales.

Cut two pieces 1¾ inches (4.4 cm) wide from the center of the plank. These pieces will have their grain most closely matched. Check them for straightness and more or less equal flex.

It is possible to cut pieces from a straight plank and have them bend after they are released from the neighboring wood. If either of the pieces you cut is not straight, cut some more from the remainder of the original plank. If you start with a straight 1 x 8 piece of lumber, you should be able to get at least two good gunwale pieces. If you can't, go back to the lumberyard. You will be out some time and maybe some money, but this is nothing

Figure 7-4. Check your gunwales
for equal flex and symmetry. This
pair was not a good match. The
gunwale on the left bowed away
from the one on the right.

compared with the time you'll lose if you try to build a straight
boat out of warped lumber.

I've only once had trouble getting my gunwales to match,
and that was with yellow pine whose grain wasn't very straight. I've
never had any problems with white pine or Western red cedar.

The gunwales on Aleut boats were tapered so that they
were about ¼ inch (6 mm) deeper in front than at the back. I suspect that this was done to balance the amount of flex in the hull
from front to back. If you taper the gunwales, cut the length down
to the final 14 foot 10 inch (451.9 cm) dimension before tapering.

Whether you taper the gunwales or not, put them face
to face and make sure that both are the same dimension. If they
are not, clamp or nail them face to face and use a plane to correct any differences. Remember, any asymmetry will give you a
warped boat. Also mark the outside of each board "front" and
"up" so you don't change their orientation later.

Spreading the Gunwales

Before you mark the gunwales for the positions of the deck beams
and the rib mortises, spread them to make sure they have the same
amount of flex. If they don't, you must plane down the stiffer board.

You will need four pieces of scrap 1 x 2 (1.9 cm by 3.8 cm
cross section) lumber to set up the shape of the deck. These
pieces of wood are your spreaders. Cut their ends at the angle
shown below, the angle at which your gunwales should slope.

If you have a sliding bevel, set it for this angle and use it to

Figure 7-5. Clamp your gunwales
face to face. The end grain of one
gunwale should mirror the end
grain of the other. Mark "forward"
and "up" on each gunwale so you
don't reverse or invert them later.

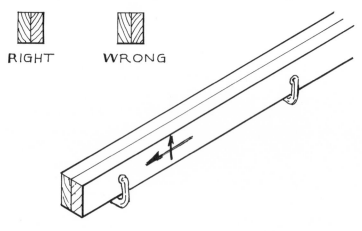

RIGHT   WRONG

mark the ends of the spreaders. If you don't, transfer this angle to a 4-inch (10 cm) piece of 1 x 2 and cut one end at this angle with a fine-tooth saw. Use this piece of wood as the bevel template to mark all the spreaders and later to check the angle on the gunwales.

The length of the spreaders should be such that the distance across the outside of the gunwales is the dimension shown below.

If you label the spreaders with the size

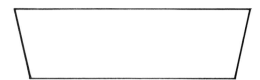

Figure 7-6. Cut the ends of the spreaders at the angle shown.

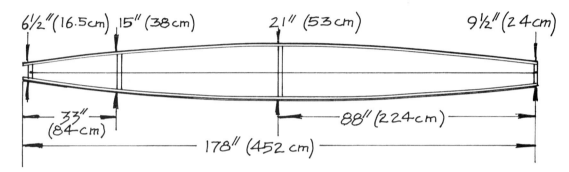

Figure 7-7. Position four spreaders as shown. The bow end of the deck is to the left.

of the boat and the distance from the end, you can reuse them on your next boat. When you are done with them, bundle them up and put them in a safe place. Otherwise, they tend to look like scrap lumber and will end up in the scrap pile.

| 21" Aleut Tail | Spreader 9½" O.D. |
| 3/4" Gunwales | |

Figure 7-8. If you mark the spreaders, your chances of using them again on your next boat will increase.

Nail the spreaders in place with some small finishing nails. If you don't drive the heads all the way in, you will be able to pull them out more easily later. I generally drill some pilot holes using one of the finishing nails as a drill bit. This makes it easier to remove the nails later.

Set the gunwales up on sawhorses and run a line from the center of the tail end to the center of the bow end. Small nails at the top center of each of the four spreaders will help with this operation. The line should pass within ⅛ inch (3 mm) of the center of the middle spreader. If it is off much farther to one side then one gunwale is stiffer than the other and you have some correcting

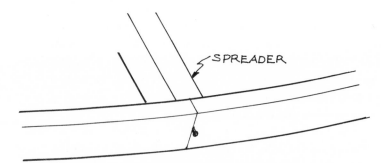

Figure 7-9. Nail the spreaders in place with small nails. Leave the heads sticking out so you can remove the nails easily when you're done.

to do. If the two gunwales are just a little off you can try to limber up the stiffer of the two by flexing it back and forth a few times. If that doesn't help, you might have to plane the stiffer of the two gunwales.

When you think the two gunwales are close enough, reassemble them with the spreaders and check the centerline one more time. If after all your efforts you still aren't happy, you might want to make another trip to the lumberyard and get some straighter lumber.

After sawing, one or both gunwales may decide to take on some twist, which you'll note by a gap between the gunwale and the spreader. Don't worry about this as long as the gunwales have equal flex and lie flat on the sawhorses. Your rib mortises will be at slightly different angles, but this is easy enough to compensate for.

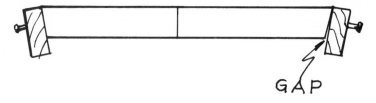

Figure 7-10. Twisting of the gunwales will show up as a small gap between the gunwales and the spreaders. Some twisting is normal and not a concern. However, make sure that the twist is not induced by unlevel sawhorses.

Fitting the Foot Brace and Back Brace

If you number the deck beams or thwarts of the Aleut kayak starting at the bow, beam number 3 is the foot brace, beam number 4 is the knee brace, and beam number 5 is the back brace. To set the position of these beams to fit your body, fix the position of the knee brace and then position the foot brace and back brace relative to the knee brace.

To find out where to position the foot brace and the back

brace, measure the distance from the balls of your feet to the back of your knees and the distance from the balls of your feet to the small of your back. You'll need two pieces of 1 x 2 about 2 feet (61 cm) long, a tape measure or yardstick, and a 4-foot (122 cm) piece of rope or strong string.

When you measure yourself for fitting into the kayak, wear the shoe and sock combination you'll wear in your boat. In the summer I paddle barefoot. When it's cold I wear the type of neoprene booties you can find in kayak or dive shops. Don't plan on wearing tennis shoes with pronounced heels or strap-on sandals in a boat with ribs. These can get caught on the ribs and make entry and exit problematic. Getting trapped in your kayak after a capsize can be potentially lethal. Also keep the thickness of your clothing in mind. A couple of sweaters and a jacket can add a half-inch or more to your back.

When you have all the necessary stuff together, sit on the floor with your back against a door. (Walls usually have baseboards, which will throw the measurements off.) Slide back so the small of your back touches the door, and move your legs together so your heels touch and your feet flop to either side at a comfortable angle. Your knees should be straight out but may be slightly flexed.

Tie the rope around the center of one of the 1 x 2s. Position the 1 x 2 at the balls of your feet and hold it in place with the rope. This is your pretend foot brace. Now you can measure and record the distance from your foot brace to the small of your back. If your feet are larger than size 11 you may also want to measure the distance from the floor to the tips of your toes and the distance across your feet to make sure that your feet will fit in the boat.

Now put the other 1 x 2 just behind your kneecaps. Hold it down with one hand and push up with your knees to simulate bracing against the knee brace. If the 1 x 2 is touching your kneecaps move it back half an inch or so until it feels comfortable. Now measure the distance between the back of the foot brace and the front of the knee brace and record it. The positioning of the knee brace is important if you expect to roll your kayak.

Figure 7-11. Seat yourself against a wall and measure the distance from your back to the balls of your feet, 1, as well as the distance from the balls of your feet to the back of your knees, 2. If you will be paddling with shoes or boots, wear your paddling boots when measuring, otherwise you will end up making your boat too tight.

Figure 7-12. Deck beams are
numbered from 1 to 7, with beam
number 1 closest to the bow. Deck
beam 3 is the foot brace, deck
beam 4 is the knee brace, and deck
beam 5 is the back brace. Letters A
through F are keyed to the text.

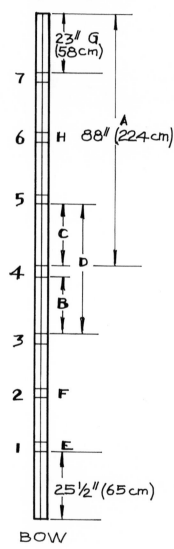

Marking the Deck Beam Positions

Once you're satisfied that your gunwales will give you a symmetrical deck, take out the spreaders, clamp the gunwales face to face, and set them on sawhorses for marking.

The instructions that follow assume you have decided not to alter the length of the boat. If you have decided to cut the gunwales either longer or shorter than the standard 14 feet 10 inches (451.9 cm), you need to proportion the measurements that follow.

The instructions that follow are keyed to Figure 7-12.

A. Measure 88 inches (224 cm) from the back end of the gunwales and mark it. This is the back of the knee brace. Mark 1½ inches (3.8 cm) in front of this mark for the front edge of the knee brace.

B. Measure forward from the front of the knee brace and mark the back of the foot brace position that you measured off your body. Mark the front of the foot brace 1½ inches (3.8 cm) ahead of that.

C. Mark 24 inches (61 cm) behind the back edge of the knee brace to be the front of the back brace. If the distance from the back of the knee brace to the small of your back as measured earlier exceeds 24 inches (61 cm) mark that dimension to the rear of the back of the knee brace. Mark 1½ inches (3.8 cm) behind that for the back of the back brace.

D. The distance from the back of the foot brace to the front of the back brace must be at least as great as the distance from the small of your back to the balls of your feet.

E. Deck beam number 1 is positioned 25½ inches (65 cm) from the front end of the gunwales.

F. Deck beam number 2 is positioned halfway between deck beam number 1 and the foot brace.

G. Deck beam number 7 is positioned 23 inches (58 cm) from the end of the gunwales.

H. Deck beam number 6 is positioned halfway between deck beam number 7 and the back brace. Mark both the front and the back of each deck beam position so that later you don't end up putting the beams on the wrong side of a mark. If you use 2 x 4s (lumber with 3.8-cm x 8.9-cm cross section) for your deck beams, space the marks 1½ inches (3.8 cm) apart.

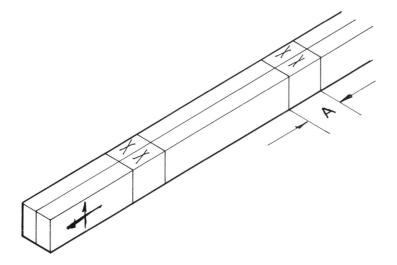

Figure 7-13. Mark the position of the deck beams on the tops and sides of the gunwales. Dimension A represents the width of the deck beam. Mark both front and back of each deck beam position so you don't accidentally install a deck beam on the wrong side of a line.

Marking the Rib Mortises

There will be one rib centered on each of the deck beams, with the remaining ribs spaced evenly in between about 4 inches (10 cm) apart. Ribs start 4 inches (10 cm) from the front of the gunwales and end 4 inches (10 cm) from the back.

    With the gunwales still clamped together, turn them over so the bottom edges face up. Use a square to make a line across both gunwales at each rib mortise position.

    Start by marking a line centered on each deck beam. Ribs in between the deck beams should be spaced about 4 inches (10

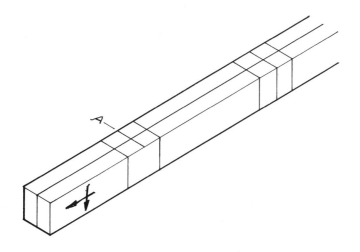

Figure 7-14. Mark the position of rib mortises on the underside of the gunwales at the center of each of the deck beam marks, A.

cm) apart. In between the back brace and the knee brace, which will be where you sit, put in an extra rib to give you a spacing more like 3½ inches (8.9 cm). This will make for more comfortable seating.

If you get an odd distance like 18½ inches (47 cm), which does not divide nicely by 4, space the ribs a little closer than 4 inches (10 cm) apart. Rather than doing elaborate arithmetic to decide what 18½ inches (47 cm) divided by 5 comes to, use some part of your hand that is slightly less than 4 inches (10 cm) and mark off five equal spaces. Once you have found the right part of your hand to use, make your marks and then go back and remark them with a square.

Once you have marked all the rib positions, set your scribe for half the thickness of the gunwales, somewhere around ⅜ inch (1 cm). Run down the length of each gunwale and mark the center of the gunwale at each rib position. Make sure you mark both gunwales by running a scribe along the outside face of the gunwales in case your scribe mark isn't exactly centered or your gunwales vary in thickness along their length.

Drilling the Rib Mortises

Once you have marked the rib mortise positions, you are ready to drill. Rib mortises are holes ⅜ inch (10 mm) in diameter and ½ inch (13 mm) deep. Wrap a piece of tape around the drill bit to mark the ½-inch (13 mm) depth.

Figure 7-15. You can use your hand to space rib mortises evenly.

Drill the mortises at the positions you marked. Keep the holes vertical.

Carving the Spirit Line

Aleut kayaks of early construction had spirit or life lines carved on the inside face of the gunwales. The spirit line is like the digestive tract, the circulatory system, and the nervous system of an animal all rolled into one. Since a kayak is a living thing, it needs a spirit line. The spirit line is a shallow groove that runs the length of the gunwales, about ¾ inch (1.9 cm) up from the bottom of the gunwales.

It seems that baidarkas built in the 20th century no longer had spirit lines. The disappearance of the spirit line seems to go hand in hand with a general decline in decoration on the boats. However, I put them on my boats and you are naturally free to put them on yours.

Set Up the Deck Again

You are now done working on the gunwales and are ready to start assembling the deck.

Put the spreaders back in place and set the gunwales up on sawhorses. Run a string down the center of the boat as before to check for symmetry.

Also check that both sawhorses are parallel. More important, check that the tops of both sawhorses are level. If they aren't, shim them up to level them. If the sawhorses aren't level you will put twist into the deck, which you will tend to lock in with the deck beams.

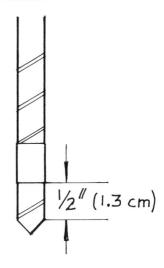

Figure 7-16. Use a piece of tape on your drill to mark the depth to which you will drill the rib mortises.

½″ (1.3 cm)

Figure 7-17. A view of the spirit line carved on the inside of the gunwales.

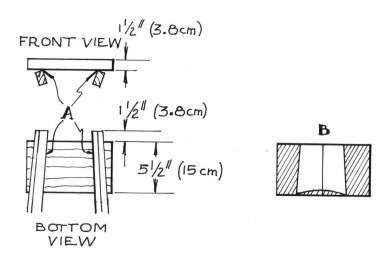

Figure 7-18. Lay the blank for the bow cross block across the gunwales and mark on the inside of the gunwales, A. Cut away the shaded portions shown in drawing B.

FRONT VIEW

1½" (3.8cm)

A

1½" (3.8cm)

5½" (15 cm)

BOTTOM VIEW

B

The Bow and Stern Cross Blocks

The bow and stern cross blocks join the gunwales at either end of the boat. Each is made in one piece and then cut in half. The halves are then lashed back together. It would seem simpler just to leave the cross blocks in one piece, but I suspect they were cut and then relashed to let them move as the hull twisted in a heavy sea.

Shaping the Bow Block

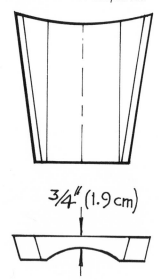

Figure 7-19. Bottom view and front view of the bow cross block with the underside scooped out.

¾" (1.9 cm)

Cut the bow block from a piece of lumber with a 1½-inch x 5½-inch (3.8 cm by 14 cm) cross section. Cut a slightly oversized piece and place it across the gunwales for marking. (See Figure 7-18 for details.) When marking the bow block, make sure you lay it on top of the gunwales, which is where they are at their widest.

Make the block just a little wider than you marked it to compensate for the width of the center saw cut.

Cut or carve the board so it has the right shape as viewed from the top. Cut the taper on the sides of the block to match the angle of the gunwales. Scoop out the underside of the block.

Mark and drill the lashing holes. Make sure they are aligned, because if they aren't your gunwales won't line up.

Once you have drilled the holes, cut some channels between the holes both at the top and at the bottom of the block. These channels will ensure that the lashings stay below the surface of the block. If they stick up, they will be cut through by the deck stringer.

Peg the bow block to the gunwales using ¼-inch (6 mm) dowels. Do not cut the bow block in two halves yet.

The Stern Block

Cut a slightly oversized blank from a piece of lumber with a 1½-inch by 5½-inch (3.8 cm by 14 cm) cross section.

Put the blank across the gunwales and mark it. Notice that this block goes past the end of the gunwales by about 1 inch (2.5 cm).

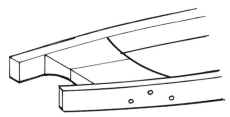

Figure 7-20. Drill lashing holes in the bow cross block 2 inches (5 cm) from the front edge and dowel it to the gunwales with three dowels.

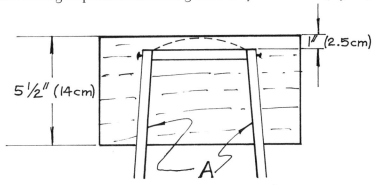

Cut the block so it has the right shape when viewed from above. Do not taper the sides to match the angle of the gunwales the way you did with the bow block. The angle on the stern block is 90 degrees, which will make each half stick up at the angle of the gunwales.

Scoop out the underside of the block. Mark the centerline and cut the block in equal halves. Peg the halves to the gunwales. Make sure they stay aligned.

Cut off the excess wood so the faces of the cut mate up evenly. Drill holes, cut a channel so the lashings don't protrude, and lash.

Cutting the Bow Block

With the stern block in place, you can cut the bow block in half. Once cut, you need to lash

Figure 7-21. Bottom view of the gunwales with the blank for the stern cross blocks laid across them for marking. Mark the blank on the inside of the gunwales, A. Remember to leave 1 inch (2.5 cm) of overhang at the end.

Figure 7-22. Dimensions of the stern cross block. You will need to cut it in half before doweling the halves to the gunwales. Unlike the bow cross block, which has sloping sides, the stern cross block has straight sides.

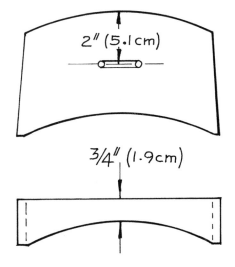

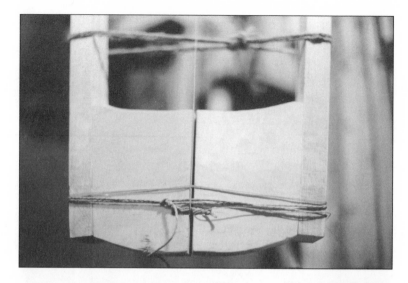

Figure 7-23. View of the stern cross blocks after doweling to the gunwales. The gap between the blocks will disappear after the mating surfaces have been planed to fit flush.

Figure 7-24. View of the finished installation of the stern cross blocks. The ends of the cross block have been planed so they mate up flush.

the halves together. Again, make sure the lashings don't stick up above the channel you cut for them.

A Few Words about Deck Beams

There are two ways to join the deck beams to the gunwales: mortise-and-tenon construction or doweled butt joint construction. Both are diagrammed in Figure 7-26.

I have used both and prefer the doweled butt joint

Figure 7-25. View of the finished installation of the bow cross blocks.

method because it is faster. The methods seem to be equally strong. The doweled butt joint requires that you pay constant attention to the alignment of the deck beams and the gunwales, while the mortise-and-tenon is essentially self-aligning.

Doweled butt joint construction is described below, and mortise-and-tenon construction is covered in Appendix 3.

Sizing the Deck Beams

With the deck spread and the bow and stern crosspieces in place, you are ready to put in the deck beams. With the doweled

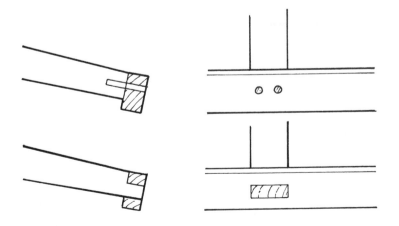

Figure 7-26. The top pair of drawings shows a cross section and an end view of a deck beam doweled into the gunwales. The bottom pair of drawings shows the same views for a deck beam joined to the gunwales via mortise-and-tenon construction.

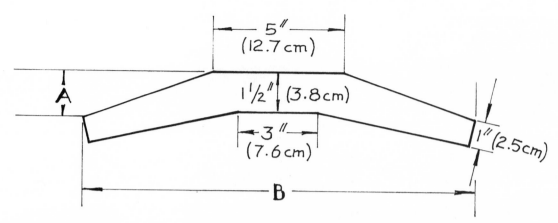

5″
(12.7 cm)

A

1½″ (3.8 cm)

3″
(7.6 cm)

1″ (2.5cm)

B

Figure 7-27. Deck beam dimensions. Dimension A is the elevation of the deck beam above the gunwales. Dimension B is the inside distance between the gunwales.

construction, each beam is measured, fit, cut, and doweled in place before the next one is cut and fit. The dimensions of the deck beams are shown above. The elevation of the deck beams is greatest at the cockpit and decreases toward the bow and the stern. The beams fit inside the gunwales. The top of each beam on the Hearst Museum boat is about ¼ inch (6 mm) below the top of the gunwales. You can also locate the tops of the deck beams flush with the tops of the gunwales and gain ¼ inch (6 mm) of interior space.

Cut your deck beams from knot-free sections of 2 x 4s; that is, lumber with a 1½-inch (3.8 cm) by 3½-inch (8.9 cm) cross section. Cut the length of the 2 x 4 to the widest part of the inside

Figure 7-28. Mark the width of each deck beam by laying the stock across the gunwales and marking from underneath.

width at the top of the gunwales. Then mark the 2 x 4s as shown in Figure 7-28.

Once you have marked the deck beam dimensions on the 2 x 4, you need to remove the unwanted wood. I use an adze, which gets me to between ⅟₁₆ and ⅛ inch (1.5 to 3 mm) of the lines, then I use a plane and a crooked knife to do the final smoothing. If you have access to a band saw, the process is much faster.

Once the unwanted wood is removed, all that's left is to trim the ends of the deck beam to match the slope of the gunwales. I use my fine-tooth backsaw or dovetail saw to do the cutting, and I do the final adjustment with a chisel or knife. Make sure your tools are sharp because end grain tends to crush or splinter if they aren't.

When the deck beam fits, fix it in place with some fourpenny finishing nails. These are thin nails, about 1½ inches (3.8 cm) long. This will prevent the beam from slipping when you drill the holes for the dowels.

Before you drill the dowel holes, sight down your deck and make sure it is still aligned. If it is, go ahead and drill two holes with your ¹⁵⁄₆₄-inch drill bit into each end of the deck beam. The holes should go through the gunwale and about 2 inches (5 cm) into the deck beam. Cut your ¼-inch (6 mm) dowel rod slightly longer than the holes and pound them in place. (If you use metric drills, experiment between drill and dowel combinations until you get a hole just slightly smaller than your dowels.)

Drill and dowel one hole at a time, then drill and dowel the next and so on. If you drill all the holes first and then dowel them, you risk some of the holes being misaligned.

Do not use glue on the dowels. You want them to have some freedom of movement when the boat is under stress.

Fitting the Knee Brace and Backrest

The two deck beams that function as the knee brace and back brace also support the cockpit coaming. Both of these beams have an elevation of 2¼ inches (5.7 cm) above the tops of the gunwales. Shape them and put them in place as described above. Put the knee brace in place first. You'll have to remove the center spreader to do this. Fit the backrest and nail it in place. Before you dowel it, measure the inside diagonals between the two deck

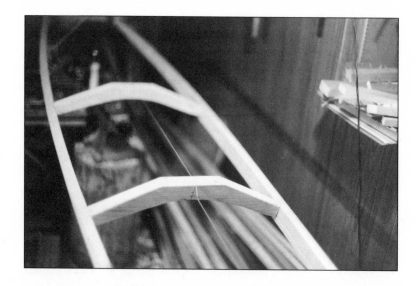

Figure 7-29. When the first two deck beams are in place, you are ready to set the elevation for the remaining deck beams.

beams. Both diagonals should be the same. If they aren't, slide the gunwales forward or backward relative to each other until both diagonals are the same. Then dowel the backrest.

Determining the Elevation of the Remaining Deck Beams

Once the backrest and the knee brace are in place, you can determine the elevation of the remaining deck beams. With the gunwales supported on the sawhorses, check their sheer. The gunwales should be about 1½ inches (3.8 cm) lower at the cockpit area than at the ends. Move the sawhorses if need be to get the right amount of sheer, out toward the ends for more, or in toward the middle for less.

Once you are happy with the sheer, run a string or a spare piece of wood from ½ inch below the top of the foot brace to the top of the gunwales at the bow. At each of the front deck beam

Figure 7-30. After the first two deck beams are in place, string a line ½ inch (13 mm) below the top of each deck beam to the ends to set the elevation B for the other deck beams. Position the sawhorses so the elevation at A is about 1 inch (2.5 cm) lower than at the ends. Also make sure that the tops of both sawhorses are level.

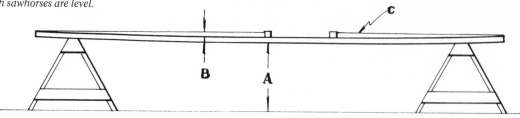

positions, measure the distance between the tops of the gunwales and the string or piece of wood. This will be the elevation of each of those deck beams. Write down the elevations for each deck beam on the gunwale. Repeat the same process for the two deck beams in back of the cockpit.

Figure 7-31. Use a small nail to keep the string ½ inch (13 mm) below the top of the deck beam.

Fitting the Remaining Deck Beams

Now that you have the elevations of the remaining deck beams, mark them, cut them, fit them, and dowel them in place. As you put each additional deck beam in place, recheck the alignment of the gunwales to make sure you aren't pulling them out of line as you're pegging them in place.

Breaking the Edges

Now is a good time to break any sharp edges on your deck. Use the spokeshave or block plane. One pass with the spokeshave is sufficient. Pay special attention to the upper outside edge of the deck beam, which is the edge that the skin will be pulled over. Also make sure the undersides of the knee brace and foot brace

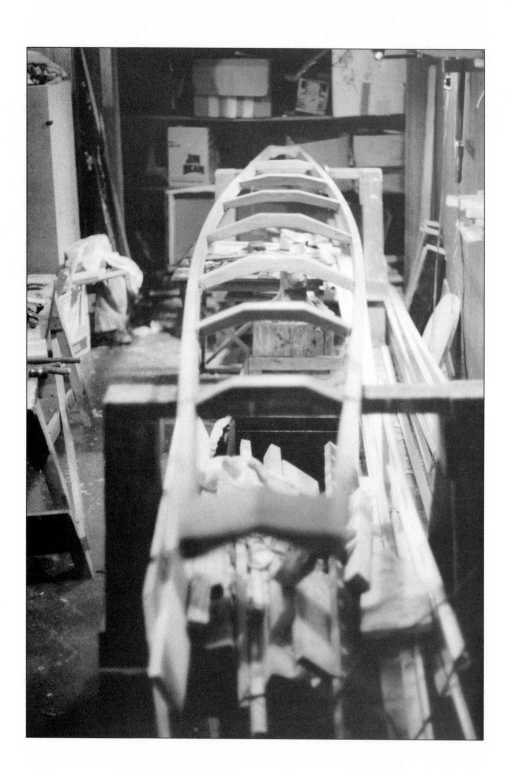

are smooth and well rounded. This is especially important if you paddle barefoot and in shorts in warm weather.

Cut any protruding dowels flush with the gunwales. If you find pencil lines and other marks offensive, also remove them at this time.

Drilling the Lashing Holes in the Deck Beams

Once all the deck beams are in place, you are ready to drill the lashing holes. Drill a ¼-inch (6 mm) hole in each deck beam approximately 2 inches (5 cm) from the inside of the gunwales. The hole should be positioned back of the center of the deck beam, otherwise your lashings will go right over the rib mortise, which is also centered on the deck beam.

Make a shallow groove in the outside edges of the gunwales at the place where the lashings will go around them. Do

(Opposite Page) Figure 7-32. A view of the finished deck with the bow and stern cross pieces in place and the deck beams highest in the center and lowest toward the ends.

Figure 7-33. Use a spokeshave to round sharp edges on the gunwales as well as on the deck beams. Just a pass or two with the spokeshave is sufficient.

Figure 7-34. Drill the lashing hole in the deck beam off center so the lashings will not go over the rib mortise, which is centered on the deck beam.

one deck beam and lash it to make sure your holes line up before drilling the rest.

Painting the Deck Red

Aleuts stained the frames of their boats with a red ocher color, as did most of the Eskimos on the western coast of Alaska. My guess is that the red color represented the blood of the boat. Boats were considered living things with spirits of their own, so it would seem appropriate that they should also have their own blood.

I mix my own stain by squeezing an inch or two of Venetian red artist's oil color out of a tube and mixing it with an ounce or two of turpentine and boiled linseed oil. Actually, any reddish earth tone is appropriate. Red earth tones derive their color from iron oxide; so does blood.

Once you have mixed the stain, wipe it on with a rag. Rags soaked in linseed oil will catch on fire spontaneously, so take them outside when you're done and discard them in a metal garbage can away from your house or shop.

Lashing the Deck Beams

Once you have stained the deck, you are ready to lash the deck beams. Take about an armspan of string and pull it across a cake

Figure 7-35. The first loop of the lashing. Note that the lashings do not run over the rib mortise.

of beeswax until it is nice and sticky. The beeswax keeps the string from slipping and helps to keep the tension in your lashings. Tie a small loop in one end of the string. Double an 8-inch (20 cm) piece of wire. This will act as the sewing needle for the string. Run the needle through the hole in the deck beam from the bottom, go around the gunwales and through the loop in the other end of the string. Tighten up and run a few more turns of string through the hole and around the gunwales.

When the hole is about half filled, tie off the string and cut off the excess. Now you know how much string you need for each lashing and you can adjust the amount you cut off for most efficient use. I usually cut enough for two lashings since you always need some extra to tie the knots when you get to the end.

Oiling the Deck

Oiling the deck preserves both the wood and the lashings. For the first coat, mix two parts boiled linseed oil and one part turpentine. Do not use raw linseed oil since it takes weeks to dry. Use real turpentine if you can and not mineral spirits. Turpentine is derived from pine sap and so penetrates wood better than mineral spirits do. Paint the oil and turpentine mixture on both the wood and the lashings. When the first coat is dry, put on another coat of straight linseed oil. If you are concerned with long-term

Figure 7-36. When you have enough turns of lashing, tie off the end with a series of hitches and cut the excess.

durability, you might want to replace the second coat of linseed oil with a waterproof varnish such as a yacht spar varnish.

You could leave off staining and oiling until the whole boat is done, but the parts are more accessible before the ribs are in place. Besides, the staining and oiling gives you a chance to handle the deck and absorb its shape and admire its beauty.

Checking the Fit

Once you have all the deck beams in place, you can check whether the spacing and elevations of the knee brace and the back brace will allow you to get into the boat. To do this, take the deck off the sawhorses and prop it up on the ground with some blocks of wood so the tops of the gunwales in the cockpit area are 7 inches (18 cm) off the ground. Tie a 1½-inch (3.8 cm) piece of wood to the top of the back brace to simulate the height of the cockpit coaming.

Now step into the space between the knee brace and the back brace, sit down on the back brace, and support your weight by placing your hands on the gunwales. Straighten your legs and slide forward. Just as the tops of your thighs start jamming into the underside of the knee brace, the back of your rear should clear the back brace and you should be able to lower yourself to the ground. If at this point your rear end is still sitting on the back brace, the cockpit isn't long enough. If you absolutely can't fit, saw through the pegs or the tenons that hold the back brace to the gunwales and move the back brace back far enough so you can get into the boat.

Also, as you're sitting on the ground with your knees just forward of the knee brace, you should have enough room between the bottom of the knee brace and the tops of your legs. If your legs in back of your knees are being squeezed by the knee brace you need to make your boat a little deeper.

The Hull

Now that you've finished the deck, let's take a look at the hull. The components of your kayak hull are the ribs, the stringers, and a keelson.

The keelson is usually considered to consist of three parts, but in my opinion, the bow plate, which looks like an extension of the deck, is structurally a part of the keelson. You'll notice that it moves with the keelson, rather than with the deck. So installing the keelson consists of assembling the bow plate and the tailfin as well as the three sections of the keelson itself. All five parts are lashed to each other and also to the ribs.

Finally, the eight hull stringers are lashed to the ribs. This completes the hull. All that's left to complete the frame is the addition of the deck stringers and the cockpit coaming; we'll get to that in the next chapter.

Notching the Front of the Gunwales

Notch the front 1½ inches (3.8 cm) of the gunwales to a depth equal to the thickness of the bow plate, or ¾ inch (1.9 cm). The notches let the bow plate sit on top of the gunwales without protruding above them. See Figures 8-1 and 8-2 for details.

The Bowpiece and Tailfin

As a matter of fact, the bowpiece and the tailfin aren't really needed until all the ribs are in place and the keelson is ready to be lashed in place. I mention them now because making them is nice filler

Figure 8-1. Detailed dimensions of the notches at the bow end of the gunwales. Depth of the notches should match the thickness of the bow plate.

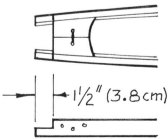

1½" (3.8cm)

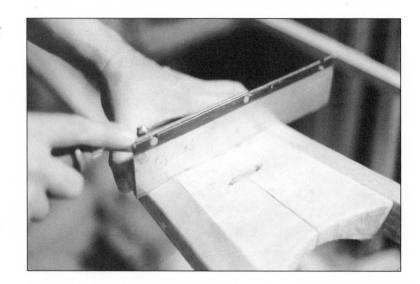

Figure 8-2. Use a small saw to cut the notches at the front of the gunwales.

Figure 8-3. Detailed dimensions for constructing the bow plate. Glue up the pieces as shown at the top and then shape them as shown at the bottom.

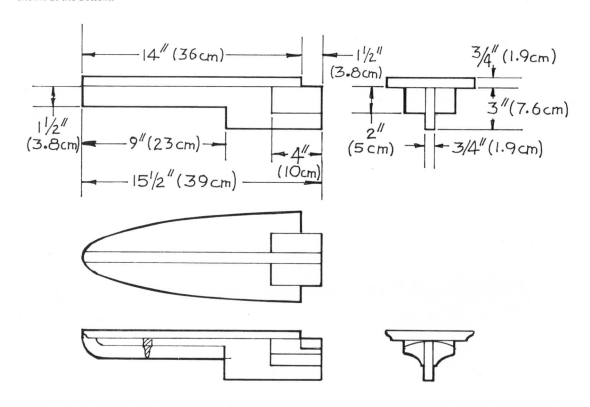

work, which you can do if you run out of ribs and can't go to get any more until the next day or the next weekend.

Making the Bowpiece

The bowpiece finishes off the front of the deck and joins the deck to the keelson. The Aleuts most likely carved this piece out of a single block of wood. However, gluing up the bowpiece out of smaller pieces of wood is easier if you have some clamps. This method of construction is shown below.

Start with a piece of wood that is as wide as the distance across the gunwales at the notch, about 14 inches (36 cm) long, and ¾ inch (1.9 cm) thick. Mark it so that it forms a smooth transition from the gunwales to its point. You can make fine adjustments to the shape later.

Figure 8-4. *A view of the bow plate in place at the bow cross blocks. Note the matching curvature of the two pieces. They will slide against each other as the boat flexes.*

Cut the piece that goes under the bow plate as shown in Figure 8-3. Glue it to the underside of the bow plate. If you don't have any clamps, glue it, drive some temporary nails, peg it, and then wrap it in string or bungee cords or anything that will keep some pressure on it long enough for the glue to set. Use epoxy or other waterproof glue.

Glue two blocks on either side of the vertical piece. When the glue is dry, carve them as shown in Figure 8-4.

Making the Tailfin

The tailfin joins the deck to the keelson. This requires a rather wide piece of wood. I usually glue up two pieces to save myself a trip to the lumberyard.

Carve the tailfin as shown in Figure 8-6.

The bottom of the tailfin needs to be matched to the top of the keelson, so don't do a final shaping until the keelson is in place. The notch at the front of the tail mates up with the stern cross block. The height of the tail above the notch depends on the elevation of the deck stringer. Lay a piece of wood that you will use for the deck stringer on top of the deck beams. See where it meets up with the tailpiece and mark the height of the tailpiece

Figure 8-5. You can glue up the blank for the tailpiece from narrower pieces if you have enough clamps.

Figure 8-6. Cut the tailfin as shown. An optional four-finger-wide hole in the middle of the tailfin reduces overall weight.

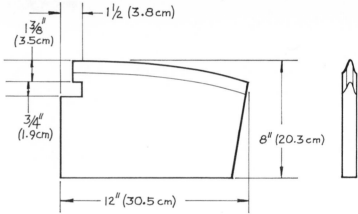

accordingly. Figure 8-7 shows the completed assembly, which gives you an idea how it will look after all the pieces are in place.

The Shape of the Hull

As you put ribs into the boat, you'll see the outline of a hull appearing. Keep in mind that this is not the final shape of the hull. The skin will be held another ⅜ inch farther out by the stringers.

In the area between the keelson and the bottommost stringer the skin will bridge the gap to form a broad V. When the

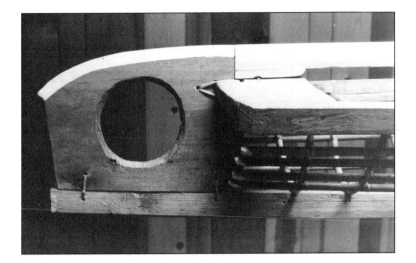

Figure 8-7. The top of the tailfin will line up with the deck stringer and the bottom will mate up with the keelson.

boat is in the water, the pressure of the water will push on the skin and make this a concave V. Figure 8-8 shows a completed hull to give you some indication of the shape you are working toward.

Figure 8-8. This is how the hull will look by the end of this chapter.

The Strength of the Hull

The hull of the Aleut kayak is a wonderful example of economical engineering. It's just strong enough to do the job—and no stronger.

You'll see that the longitudinal stringers are lashed to the ribs, which are spaced roughly 4 inches (10 cm) apart. The diameter of both the ribs and the stringers is ⅜ inch (10 mm). When the hull is subjected to stress, it is important for both ribs and stringers to have the same amount of flex. If you make the ribs substantially stronger than the stringers or vice versa, the weaker of the two will break when stress is applied. If you make the ribs and the stringers roughly the same strength, the two will have a greater chance of flexing out of the way of harm as a unit. That way, individual components are less likely to get damaged.

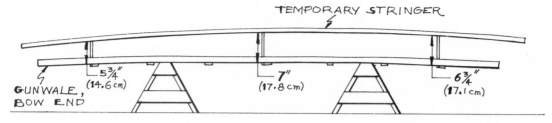

TEMPORARY STRINGER

GUNWALE, BOW END

5¾" (14.6 cm)

7" (17.8 cm)

6¾" (17.1 cm)

Figure 8-9. Elevation of the temporary stringer should be as shown. Make sure sawhorses are level before starting.

Figure 8-10. Measure the height of supports for the temporary stringer from the top of a piece of wood held underneath the gunwales.

Setting up a Form for the Ribs

With the deck inverted on the sawhorses, check once again that the sawhorses are level and parallel. Check again that you have about 1½ inches (3.8 cm) of sheer. With the deck inverted and the sawhorses far apart, the sheer has a tendency to disappear, so you might have to move the sawhorses closer together.

Using a 16-foot (488 cm) length of wood, possibly some left over from cutting your gunwales, set up a temporary stringer that will mark the elevation of the ribs. It should be about ¾ inch x 1½ inches (1.9 cm x 3.8 cm) in cross section. Its elevation should be as shown in Figure 8-9. Measure elevations from the underside of the gunwales to the top of the support as shown in Figure 8-10.

You should set the basic shape of the stringer, using a block of wood at the front of the foot brace and one block at each of the end beams. Clamp support blocks as shown in Figure 8-11.

Put additional support at the other deck beams without disturbing the curvature of the stringer. Several wraps of string at each deck beam should be sufficient. When you put in the ribs, they will be pushing up at the stringer, so you need something to hold it down. After you have added all your support, sight down the stringer to make sure it doesn't have any dips or bulges. If it does, adjust your supports or lashings as necessary.

Now that you've got all the supports in place, measure from the gunwales to the stringer to make sure it is centered. Also check

again the key elevations of the stringer, because you are now ready to start putting in the ribs.

Choosing Rib Material

Aleuts made the ribs of their baidarkas with a round cross section. If you use willow shoots or other slender branches, you get the round cross section without further effort. But if you cut your rib

Figure 8-12. With all the supports in place, the temporary stringer should form a smooth curve.

stock with a table saw, the ribs will naturally be square or rectangular in cross section. If you do it this way, you'll have to round off the edges with a spokeshave to get a round or oval cross section.

In this chapter, I'll describe ribs made from willow branches since this is the easier way to go. Steaming and bending of sawed ribs is described in Appendix 2.

Gathering Rib Stock

I use willow shoots of ½ inch (13 mm) diameter for my rib stock. Basket makers gather them in the winter, when the wood is most stable. In the springtime and early summer, new wood on the outer layer of the twig is not yet firmly attached to the inner layers and tends to delaminate when you bend it. Nevertheless, if you are ready to put ribs on your boat, gather your stock and bend

(Below left) Figure 8-13. Harvesting in the willow patch. (Robert Boucher photo)

(Below right) Figure 8-14. Ideal size of ribs is ½-inch (13 mm) diameter at the thick end with the bark on. (Robert Boucher photo)

your ribs regardless of the season. The nice thing about spring ribs is that the sap is flowing and the bark peels without any effort.

Don't pick your twigs more than a week in advance or they will dry up and become brittle. You can set them upright in a bucket of water to prolong their useful life. But if you leave them for two weeks or more, they'll send out roots below the waterline and sprout new branches above. That doesn't make for nice, smooth ribs.

My advice is to pick a few more twigs than you will need to do half a boat. When you have used those up, go pick some more.

Actually, any twig, branch, or shoot that is reasonably straight and bends uniformly is suitable for rib stock. I have used all kinds of tree and bush branches. The only twigs you should avoid are twigs with large pith cores or too many side branches.

Even if a twig isn't completely straight, it usually evens out quite a bit when you bend it. You don't necessarily need absolutely straight stock. Experiment and see what works for you.

Remember, your twigs need to be at least ⅜ inch (10 mm) in diameter when peeled, so pick them thicker to start with. Also remember that this is the minimum diameter at the thin end of the stick, which means that other end of the stick will be thicker. Thicker ribs will be stronger, of course, but they are also harder to bend to the correct shape. I find that ½ inch (13 mm) is the upper

Figure 8-15. You can use just about any stick for ribs. However, if you have a choice, avoid sticks with a large pith core (top). Sticks with a smaller pith core (bottom) are preferable.

Figure 8-16. Flex the ribs with the bark on to limber them up and to check for stiff spots.

Figure 8-17. Before you peel the rib, see how long it needs to be, and trim it slightly longer than you need.

limit on a peeled twig. Any thicker and it gets really hard to work. Take my advice and stick to peeled diameters between ⅜ (10 mm) and ½ inch (13 mm). You won't regret it.

Putting in the Ribs

Start inserting the ribs in the cockpit area of your boat. Expect to replace a few, especially since your worst work will be at the beginning and most visible in the cockpit area.

Select a twig of suitable length and with the bark still on, bend it in place. You'll take the bark off before they're permanently installed. Start with some skinnier twigs since these are easier to bend to the right shape. Use your thumbs to work the tight bends to avoid cracking the ribs. If you have not let the bark dry out, the twig should bend easily and not require any steaming. Bending without steam is the main appeal of green twigs. The downside of green twigs is that you have to peel them—but even that can be an enjoyable activity if you're in the right frame of mind.

If you pick your twigs in the spring or early summer, they will have a lot of sap under the bark and you will be able to peel them almost as easily as a banana. If you pick your twigs later in the year, the bark may be a little harder to get off. I use a crooked knife to peel them. I find that a slightly dull knife seems to work better than a really sharp one.

It's important to get all the bark off, not just the dark outer

(Opposite Page) Figure 8-18. Peel the ribs using a knife that is not too sharp. Ribs gathered in spring and early summer peel more easily than ribs gathered at any other time.

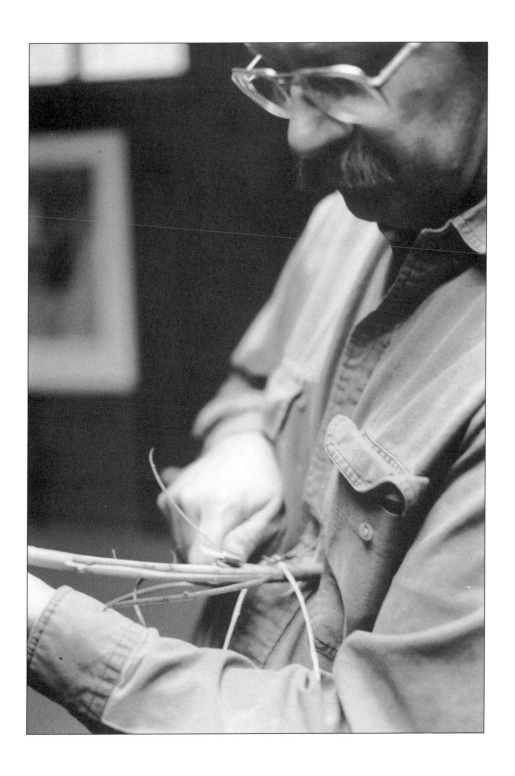

Figure 8-19. After you have trimmed the rib to length, insert the ends in their mortises and push the rib into an upright position.

bark, but also the light-colored inner bark. Any bark left on the ribs will eventually peel off on its own. If you varnish your ribs, the peeling bark will carry the varnish with it and your ribs will lose their waterproofing. That will shorten the life of the boat.

After you have pre-bent your rib and peeled it, trim it so it's even with the bottom of the gunwale or maybe ½ inch (13 mm) longer.

Whittle the ends down to fit the mortises and do the final

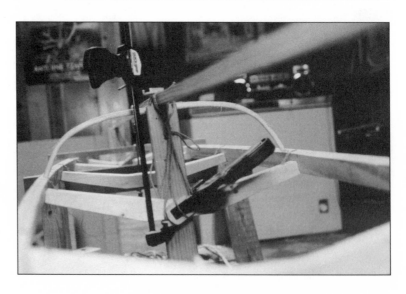

Figure 8-20. When you get the first rib in place, go to the end of the boat and check it for symmetry. Ribs near the cockpit should be flat in the middle and curved at the sides.

Figure 8-21. Two ribs down and 40 to go!

fitting. You don't have to jam the ribs tightly into the mortises. As a matter of fact, it appears that rib diameter on the original Aleut boats was about ⅟₁₆ inch (1.5 mm) less than their mortises. If they fit too tightly, they're more likely to shear off or get fatigue cracks as the boat flexes repeatedly. After you've fixed the end of the rib in its mortise, go to the end of the boat and check the rib by eye for symmetry.

Your green twigs have some taper to them, so you can either whittle them down to uniform diameter with the spoke-shave or put them in so the thicker end alternates from side to side. If you put all the ribs in with the thick end to the same side, you're likely to get a lopsided hull.

The shape of the ribs in the center of the boat should be flat in the middle and rounded at the sides as shown in Figure 8-20. As you get closer to the ends of the boat, the ribs become more arched as shown in Figures 8-22 and 8-23.

Make sure you have enough flat area in the center or you will end up with a boat that is tippy.

Put in a few more ribs on either side of the first one and check your work by eye again. Not only does each rib have to be symmetrical, but it must also make a smooth transition with the other ribs. Use a flexible batten laid across the ribs to make sure some of them don't stick up higher or sit lower than others. Either trim the nonconformists or replace them.

Figure 8-22. The shape of the ribs from the cockpit, looking forward.

Incidentally, here's a tip I've found helpful: When you put in ribs, try to give yourself enough time to do at least eight in a batch. They tend to be more uniform if you do them together.

Take time to assess your work after each session and don't be afraid to redo a section of ribs if they don't look right to you. On the other hand, don't be too critical of small irregularities. Remember, you're working with natural materials. No matter how skillful you are, your boat's not going to end up looking

Figure 8-23. The shape of the ribs from the cockpit, looking backward.

(Opposite Page) Figure 8-24. All the ribs except the last few at either end are in place.

like injection-molded plastic. But that doesn't mean it's in any way inferior in terms of strength or seaworthiness; and it will be vastly superior in terms of aesthetic appeal. Your boat will have a soul.

Work outward in both directions from the center. Put in all but the last four ribs on either end. Wait until you have the keelson in place before putting these last ribs in on either end, to make sure of the correct elevation.

Green sticks will shrink some as they dry. So, if they're tight up against the temporary keel batten when wet, they might be loose when dry. Keep this in mind when you go a day or two between sections of ribs. Don't put the green ribs in loose to match the dry ones. Put them in snug and they'll shrink to the same height as the dry ones.

When you have all but the few end ribs in place, remove the batten you used as a template for the height of the ribs and stain the ribs red.

Setting up the Keelson

Once the ribs are in place, you are ready to install the keelson.

It comes in three pieces that you assemble with dropleaf scarfs held together by lashing. The scarfs are aligned so they are supported by one of the ribs that is centered on a deck beam.

Some people who build baidarkas make the keelson in one piece, since this saves labor. I always make my keelson in three pieces because I believe that the Aleuts knew what they were doing. They would certainly have made a one-piece keelson if they had felt it was cleverer, or stronger, or safer.

A three-piece keelson with lashed scarfs will definitely behave differently from a one-piece keelson. The lashed joints have some freedom of movement and so will not propagate stresses along the bottom of the boat in the same way that a one-piece keelson would. You can test this for yourself. When your frame is all done and lashed, pick it up by one end. Flex it, twist it, shake it, and you will see how the keelson reacts to stress.

I must admit I've been tempted to make a boat with a one-piece keelson so I can see if it makes a boat behave differently on the water, but so far I haven't done so for fear of ending up with an inferior boat. Perhaps some braver soul out there would like

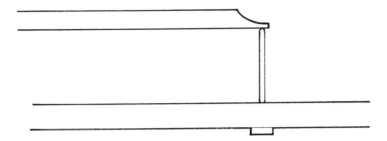

Figure 8-25. The ends of both the bow and tail sections of the keelson end in a little tail that rests on the rib, which is centered on the second deck beam from either end of the boat.

to experiment and let me know how it went.

When I put in a keelson, I generally shape the center and tail section first because they're fairly simple. I also make them longer than they need to be and don't trim them to their final length until I fit them in place. Then I fit and shape the bow section in place and lash it. When it's in place I put in the center section and then the tail section.

Given the way that the center section of the keelson is shaped, it could be dropped into place after the bow and tail sections have already been lashed. The length of the center piece could then be adjusted to fine-tune the amount of rocker and sheer in the boat. A shorter center section would make for less rocker and sheer, while a longer center section would make for more of both.

Cut the center section of the keelson from a straight piece with a 1½-inch (3.8 cm) x ¾-inch (1.9 cm) cross section. Cut it slightly too long until you can do the final fitting. The center section must reach from the second deck beam from the tail to the second deck beam from the bow. See Figure 8-26.

The center piece is the longest part of the keelson and has enough flex to assume the required curvature. However, the bow

Figure 8-26. Construction details of the center section of the keelson (top) and the tail section (bottom).

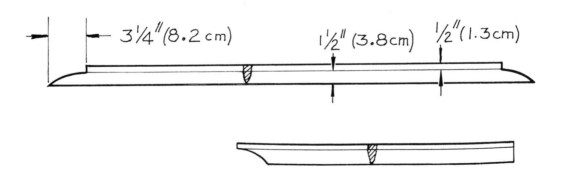

3¼" (8.2 cm)   1½" (3.8cm)   ½" (1.3cm)

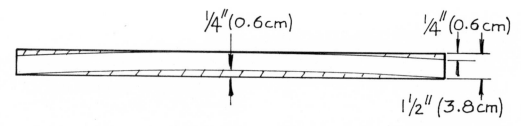

Figure 8-27. Remove shaded portions to put a ¼-inch (6 mm) curvature into the tail section of the keelson.

and tail sections of the keelson need to be *shaped* to the correct curvature.

Cut the tailpiece to the required length and a cross section of 1¾ inches (4.4 cm) by ¾ inch (1.9 cm). Then, using a plane or knife, take ¼ inch (6 mm) off the top at the end and ¼ inch (6 mm) off the bottom in the middle. See Figure 8-27.

The bowpiece has even more curvature than the tailpiece. It is most easily cut from a plank that is the right length and ¾ inch (1.9 cm) thick by 5½ inches (14 cm) or 7½ inches (19 cm) wide. If you go with the narrower board, you will have to add a piece on the nose of the keelson. If you go with the wider board, you don't have to. The long, skinny tail part of the bowpiece should start out at 2 inches (5 cm). Carve ½ inch (13 mm) of curvature into it using the same technique you used for the tailpiece.

The depth of the bow section of the keelson increases toward the front so that the first two or three ribs from the bow are shallower than the ribs following. This makes for a more gradual transition of the hull from the convex cross section of the rib area to the concave cross section in the bifurcated area of the bow.

Carving the front of the bowpiece is a little more tricky since you have to match it up to the bow plate. I do this by putting the bow plate in place and then holding the unfinished bow section of the keelson up against it so I can mark where I need to trim away wood. It generally takes me several fittings to get it right.

Figure 8-28. Detailed dimensions of the bow section of the keelson.

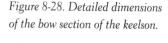

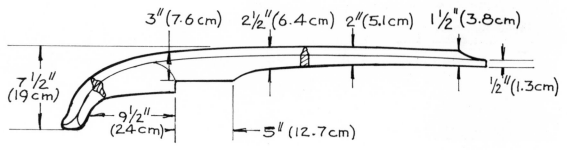

Once you have the top of the keelson matched to the bow plate, you will also need to carve the bottom edge of the keelson into a curve that sweeps gracefully upward at the bow. Remove the wood in steps and put the bow section in place on the keelson to judge the progress of your work. Stop removing wood when the curve looks right to your eye.

If you went with the narrower plank, you will now have to add a nosepiece to the bow. This piece projects about 2 inches (5 cm) above the top of the bow plate. I usually attach the nose piece with two dowels. If you make the nose too tall, it will have a tendency to break off when you turn your boat over on the beach and lift the tail to drain water out of the boat.

Once you are happy with the profile of the bow section of your keelson, you need to carve it so its cross section is as shown in Figure 8-28. The cross section of the keelson in the area of the bow is like a diamond with concave sides. This shape prevents water from being trapped under the skin and causing rot.

Putting it All Together

Fitting the keelson starts with the bowpiece. Lay it in place on the ribs and match the front up to the lower part of the bow plate. If

Figure 8-29. When you have a good match between the bow plate and the bow section of the keelson, lash the two together.

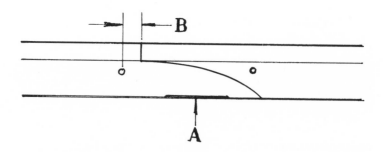

Figure 8-30. Keelson scarf detail. If distance B between the lefthand lashing hole and the edge of the keelson is too small, the keelson has a tendency to split when under stress. Remove some wood in area A of the keelson so the lashings are recessed and don't form a lump under the skin.

Figure 8-31. Lashings around the scarf hold the two sections face to face. The heavier lashings through the holes pull the two sections together. If your keel is made of soft wood, the heavy lashings saw away at the holes as you flex the boat and the keelson sections start to separate.

the match isn't exactly right, make your final adjustments now.

Lay the keelson on the ribs and see where the end lines up in respect to the rib that is centered on the second deck beam. Trim it so it extends about ¼ inch (6 mm) past the rib. Cut the scarf into the tail as shown in Figure 8-30.

Lash the keelson to the bow plate as shown in Figure 8-29.

Cut one end of the middle keelson section to match the end of the bow section. Clamp it to the bow section and cut the other end to length. Cut the scarf on it as well.

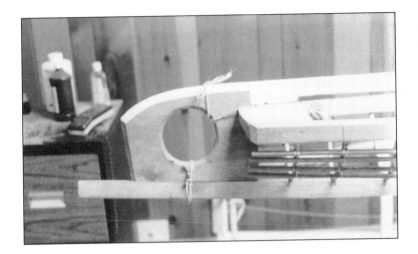

Now drill holes on either side of the scarf joints as shown in Figure 8-30. Make sure you don't drill the holes too close to the edge of the wood or the keelson will have a tendency to split between the hole and the edge if enough stress is put on the boat in use. Before you lash, carve away enough of the keelson so the lashings will not make a lump under the skin.

Lash the two sections together as shown in Figure 8-31. It might seem easier to you to lash around the scarf and then pull the two halves together. You must realize, however, that when you lash around the keelson, the pressure of the lashing has a tendency to squeeze the halves apart. So, first do the lashing that pulls the halves together. You will have to use your lashing needle to get under the lashing already in place.

Finally, match the tail section of the keelson to the center section and lash the two together. If you cut the tailfin oversized, mark it where it overlaps the keelson and cut it to match. Trial-lash the two pieces together.

Finally, install the remaining ribs in the bow and tail sections of the hull to mate up with the keelson, which is now in place.

Aligning the Keelson

The keelson needs to be straight and centered between the gunwales. If your deck is symmetrical, it will be. But if your deck isn't symmetrical, you should lay the keelson in a straight line rather than having it follow an equidistant curve between both gunwales.

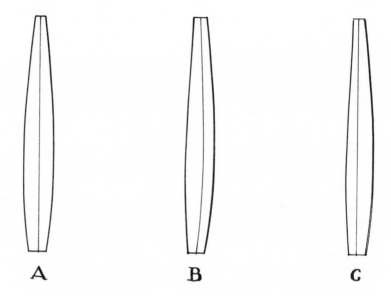

Figure 8-33. If your hull is straight, as in A, your keelson should be straight when evenly spaced between the gunwales. If your hull is slightly warped, it is better to run the keelson straight, as in C, rather than equidistant from both gunwales but curved, as in B.

A   B   C

At least, you should *try* to lay it in a straight line. In my experience, the keelson eventually seems to go where it wants, and there's practically nothing you can do about it. I had one boat where the tail section wandered off to one side after about a month of use and then recentered itself a few months later. I believe that if the parts of a boat are allowed to move relative to each other, as they are in an Aleut kayak, they will eventually align themselves in a desirable state of natural equilibrium.

Lashing the Keelson

The Aleuts used to lash the keelson to the ribs by lashing over the ridge of the keelson. The advantage of this lashing method is that it allows the keelson to slide on the ribs as the boat flexes in the waves. The main disadvantage is that sand gets between the skin and the keelson and tends to wear through the lashing.

Another disadvantage is that it allows the ribs to creep out of position over time. This wasn't a problem for the Aleuts because they could realign the ribs when they replaced the skins of their boats every year or so. It becomes a problem, though, when you have a canvas skin that can last in excess of five years.

Luckily, there's an alternate method of lashing the keelson to the ribs: Simply run the lashings through holes drilled in

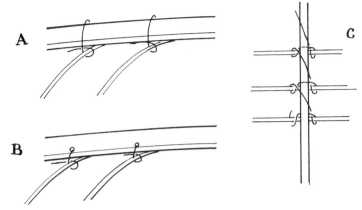

the keelson. This method avoids the problems of creeping ribs as well as abrasion of lashings. Admittedly, it does tend to fix the keelson more rigidly than the Aleut method of lashing. However, on the whole it's probably an acceptable compromise, since it saves you the trouble of stripping a perfectly good skin off the boat to realign ribs and redo the lashings.

Making the Hull Stringers

Cut the hull stringers from a 16-foot (488 cm) board to a ⅜-inch (10 mm) square cross section. I usually cut them from rough cut planks with an actual thickness of 1 inch (2.5 cm). I cut four ⅜-inch (10 mm) strips from the edge, which will then be 1 inch (2.5 cm) wide. I then cut each of those strips in half lengthwise and I have my ⅜ inch (10 mm) square dimension.

Once you've made all eight of your stringers, round the edges with your spokeshave to give them a round or elliptical cross section. You can hold the stringer with one hand and work the spokeshave with the other. When you use a spokeshave with both hands, you draw it toward yourself, but when you use it one-handed, you can either work toward or away from yourself, whichever feels more comfortable.

When you have shaped all the stringers, stain them red.

Lashing the Hull Stringers

When you've finished shaping the stringers, trial-lash them to the ribs. Space the stringers closest to the keelson about 10 inches

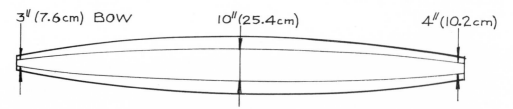

3" (7.6cm) BOW   10"(25.4cm)   4"(10.2cm)

Figure 8-35. Space the two stringers closest to the keelson as shown. Space the other stringers evenly between the gunwales and the bottommost stringers.

Figure 8-36. Trim stringers even with the ends of the gunwales and round them off so they don't poke at the skin.

(25 cm) apart at the center of the cockpit, 3 inches (7.6 cm) apart at the bow, and 4 inches (10 cm) apart at the tail. Arrange all the other stringers so they're spaced evenly between the gunwales and the stringers closest to the keelson.

Trim the stringers even with the ends of the gunwales. Taper the ends of the stringers so they won't have their edges poking into the skin.

Now lash all the stringers, starting at the gunwales and working toward the keelson. Use the lashing patterns shown in Figure 8-37. The material I use for lashing is an artificial sinew sold by Tandy Leather, which you should be able to get at any leathercraft store. It's waxed, unbraided nylon, which lies flat and doesn't cause much of a lump under the skin.

Actually, any line that lies flat, such as the old-style braided bait-casting line, would work just as well. Lashings must be tight or your boat will turn out limp and slow. However, even when they're tight, they will still allow enough movement to prevent damage, should the boat be subjected to severe stresses.

Every five ribs or so, run a lashing from the topmost stringer around the gunwale. This helps to hold the ribs into their mortises until you get the skin in place.

Checking the Fit

Now comes the exciting bit. Now you can try on your boat for fit. Take it off the sawhorses and put it on the ground. Put 2 x 4s on either side of the keelson to support the ribs while you slide into the cockpit to check the fit. If the boat is too tight, it's not too late to change it.

While you're in there imagining yourself swooping over the seas, check the position of the rib near your heels. If it sits right under your heels, move it backward or forward so it's out of the way. You don't have to do it right away. You can sit there and enjoy yourself a little longer if you like.

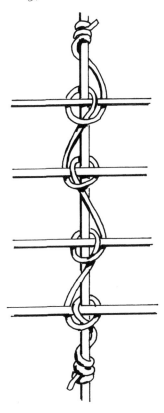

Figure 8-37. The pattern for lashing stringers to ribs. The lashing follows the rib.

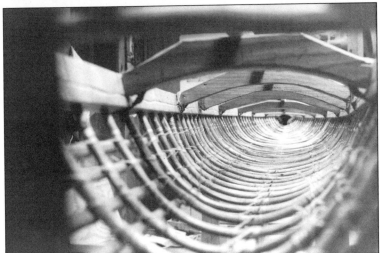

(Top Left) Figure 8-38. An occasional lashing run around the gunwales holds the ribs in their mortises when the skin is off the boat.

(Bottom Left) Figure 8-39. A final look into the belly of the completed hull.

9 Finishing the Frame

You're well on the way now. The worst part is behind you. All that's left to do on the hull is to shape and install the deck stringers, and to install the cockpit coaming. After that, I'll show you how to do the final tuning of the boat, and stain and varnish the hull.

Carving the Deck Stringers

Deck stringers can be cut from a single clear ¾-inch (1.9 cm) x 3½-inch (8.9 cm) x 8-foot (244 cm) long board or from material left over from cutting the gunwales. Cut the stringers 1⅜ inches (3.5 cm) wide. Lay them on the deck of the boat and mark them for cutting 1 to 2 inches (2 to 5 cm) longer than they need to be. You will do the final trimming later. They need to go from the bow to

Figure 9-1. The tops of the deck stringers are shaped to reduce their weight. The shape on the right is the Aleut original. The shape on the left is easier to carve, though.

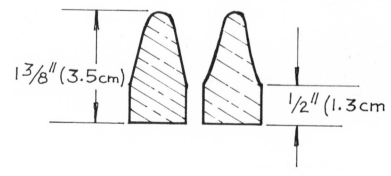

1⅜" (3.5cm)   ½" (1.3cm

the back edge of the knee brace and from the tail to the front edge of the backrest. Deck stringers are tapered at the top to reduce their weight.

Using your center scribe, run a centerline down the top edge of both stringers. Run two lines down the length of both stringers, ½ inch (13 mm) from the bottom edge. Use a plane to shape the stringers so their cross section looks as shown in Figure 9-1.

Fitting the Deck Stringers

With the kayak upright on the sawhorses, check the sheer, or upward bend, of the gunwales. Curvature should be such that the gunwales at the center of the cockpit are about 1½ inches (3.8 cm) lower than at the ends. Move the sawhorses closer together or farther apart as need be.

Put the back deck stringer in place so it butts up against the tailfin. Cut the deck stringer so the front is even with the front end of the backrest deck beam (Figure 9-3).

Put the front deck stringer in place so its back lines up with the back face of the knee brace deck stringer. Cut the front end so it comes to within 7 inches (17.8 cm) of the front of the bow plate. Round off the front of the front deck stringer as shown in Figure 9-6. Cut the cockpit end of the deck stringer as shown in Figure 9-3.

Figure 9-2. The back end of the rear deck stringer butts up against the tailfin.

Figure 9-3. The ends of the deck stringers sit on top of the deck beams that support the cockpit coaming.

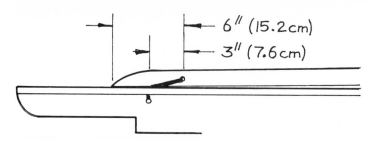

Figure 9-4. Location of deck stringer lashing holes at the bow end.

6″ (15.2cm)

3″ (7.6cm)

Figure 9-5. Lash deck stringers at each of the deck beams.

Lashing the Deck Stringers

Lash the deck stringers at each deck beam as shown in Figure 9-5. This lashing keeps the deck stringers in contact with the deck beams but still allows them to slide back and forth.

Lash the front stringer at the bow as shown in Figure 9-6. Note that the lashing hole is about 6 inches (15 cm) back from the front of the stringer. The corresponding lashing holes in the bow plate are about 3 inches (10 cm) forward of the hole in the deck stringer. I believe this arrangement gives the bow plate a greater range of movement than if the holes were aligned right on top of each other.

Making a Form for the Coaming

Your best bet for making the coaming is to cut a form out of ¾-inch (1.9 cm) plywood. Cut out the inside of the form so that it looks like a doughnut. The rim should be about 2 inches (5 cm) wide. The shape of the form should be oval to slightly egg-shaped with the pointier end toward the front. The length of the form should be the same as the distance between the knee brace and the backrest. The width of the form should be 3 inches (7.6 cm) less than the width of the kayak halfway between the knee brace and the backrest.

Figure 9-7. Steamed coamings are bent around the plywood form and clamped until dry.

Cutting the Coaming

The coaming should be ⅜ inch (10 mm) to ½ inch (13 mm) thick, 1½ inches (3.8 cm) high, and long enough to go all around the form plus another 5 inches (13 cm) longer for overlap. The wood can be anything that bends well. I have used white ash, birch, and oak. Green wood is preferable since you'll have to bend it.

Taper the last 5 inches (13 cm) on either end of the coaming for smooth overlap. Round off three of the four edges. The unrounded edge will go to the top outside of the coaming.

Bending the Coaming

Before you bend the coaming, you'll need to soak it in water for a few days. If you soak it for a week or more, it can become too soft and the fibers will separate when you bend it. If you plan to build more than one boat, you might want to go to the trouble to cap off both ends of an 8-foot section of rain gutter and use that as a soaking trough. Otherwise, a piece of plastic sheeting laid between two boards will make a nice impromptu soaking trough.

When you're done soaking the wood, it's ready to be bent. You can either steam the entire coaming for 15 minutes and then bend it around the form, or you can ladle boiling water over short sections of the coaming and bend it around the form a little at a time.

Again, the preferred method depends on whether you expect to build any more boats. If you are expecting to build more, you might want to make a steam box out of a section of downspout or sheets of foam insulation. See Appendix 2 on steam-bent ribs for more details on steaming.

Unsteamed Coamings

You can avoid steaming altogether if you make the coaming out of three layers of ⅛-inch (3 mm) wood strips instead of a single ⅜-inch (10 mm) strip. Hardwood ⅛ inch (3 mm) thick, if soaked and possibly softened with a little hot water, bends without any effort. Layer the sections so you get uniform thickness all around.
Keep them clamped to the form until dry, then drill them and lace them together. Lace another strip, ½ inch (13 mm) wide by ¼ inch (6 mm) thick, around the outside top of the coaming. This provides a lip for the spray skirt to grab onto when you're paddling. If you want a more pronounced lip, hold off adding this strip of wood until after you have put the skin on the boat.

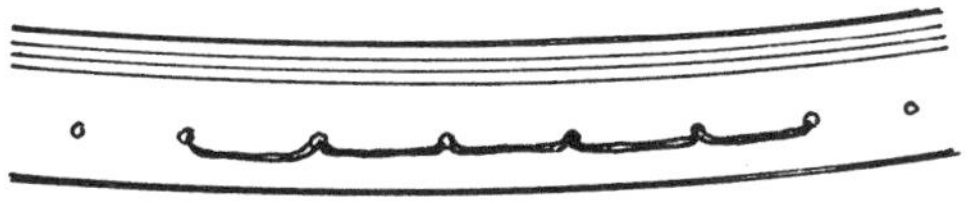

Figure 9-8. If you make your coaming out of multiple strips, drill them and lace them together.

Installing the Coaming

Line the coaming up with the deck stringers. Lash the coaming to the deck stringers and to the deck beams as shown in Figure 9-9.

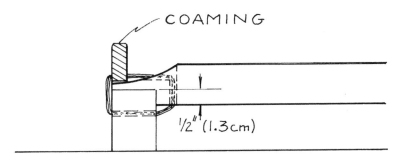

COAMING

½" (1.3 cm)

Figure 9-9. The lashing ties both the coaming and the deck stringer to the deck beam.

Figure 9-10. The tail of the deck stringer slides into a notch at the bottom of the cockpit coaming.

Notch the bottom edge of the coaming to fit over the tail ends of the deck stringers as shown in Figure 9-10.

Carving the Coaming Stanchions

The coaming stanchions support the coaming on either side of the cockpit. Stanchions should be three to four fingers wide and reach from the gunwales to the underside of the coaming. Notch both ends of the stanchions to fit the edge of the gunwale and the coaming. The grain of the stanchions should run at right angles to the gunwales.

Figure 9-11. The stanchions support the cockpit at the sides.

Drill matching holes in the stanchions, the gunwales, and the coaming. Lash them together. Keep knots on the inboard side of the stanchion to avoid lumps under the skin.

Final Trimming of the Tail Section

Now you're ready to do the final trimming and lashing of the tail section. See Figure 9-12 for details.

Fitting Storage Bags

It's obvious that any gear you stow in your kayak has to go in and out through the cockpit. The best way I've found to organize the gear is to pack it into canvas bags tailored to the inside of the kayak. Since the bags have to clear the deck beams, the best time to fit them is before the skin is on. Essentially, you want to measure the cross-sectional area at each of the deck beams and make your storage bags slightly smaller. I've found that two bags forward and one aft seem to work the best.

Seat Slats

You may want to add seat slats to provide some additional support for the mat you will be sitting on. The slats don't need to be very wide to be effective. An adequate width is 2 to 3 inches (5 to

Figure 9-12. Do the final trimming and lashing of the tail section at this point.

8 cm). I usually cut some ¾-inch (1.9 cm) thick boards in two to give me slats of ¼-inch (6 mm) to ⅜-inch (10 mm) thickness. Drill some holes in the slats and lash them to the ribs. Seat slats are best lashed under the ribs rather than on top since you'll be sitting lower that way, making the boat more stable.

Note, however, that you'll need to keep the slats close to the keelson so they won't poke into the skin. Also keep your knots small when you lash the slats to the ribs. Thick knots will also tend to poke through the skin. Remember that when the boat is in the water, the skin will be pushed even closer to the ribs.

I've also put seat slats on top of the ribs in one of my boats and find that this is less comfortable on long trips than having them below the ribs. The Aleuts apparently had no use for seat slats and I'm ready to try my next boat without them.

Staining, Oiling, and Varnishing

Now that all the parts of the frame are in place, you should apply red stain to any part of the frame you haven't stained yet. After about a day, you can apply some sort of waterproofing to the wood. A mixture of about one-third turpentine and two-thirds boiled linseed oil is a traditional nautical waterproofing medium. Polyurethane varnish, although less traditional, probably gives longer lasting protection than the linseed oil mixture. Regardless of whether you use oil or varnish, you should apply two coats for best results.

The Skin

10

Strange as it may seem, the skin is not merely a waterproof covering for the frame of the kayak—it's an important structural element as well. The skin pulls all the parts together and limits the bending of an otherwise very flexible boat.

The first rule is that the skin must be really tight. A loose skin makes for a slow, floppy boat. On the other hand, a lightweight kayak with a tight skin is a thrilling thoroughbred. It's an amazingly satisfying thing to handle. You'll feel the tension and resilience of the wood working for you as you paddle it.

In times gone by, kayaks were covered with animal skins that needed to be oiled to make them waterproof. Even then, they would start picking up water after a day or two, and need to be dried out. Within a year or so, the skin had to be replaced. The old skin was usually removed at the beginning of winter before the kayaks were put up for storage.

The canvas with which you will cover your boat is much more tolerant of moisture. As a matter of fact, if you take a trip of several days and have your boat in the water every day, you'll find that the skin gets tighter day by day. This is good up to a point, but beyond that point the tension will actually start distorting the frame. This does not mean that you should make the skin loose when you first sew it on. It simply means that when you store your kayak between trips you should give it a chance to dry out.

Canvas and Other Coverings

I've always covered my boats in canvas, although other coverings are available. In some European countries, linen is cheaper and more readily available than cotton duck. If you live there, get linen, but make sure it has a tight weave and not the looser weave sometimes sold for artist's canvases.

Other alternatives to canvas are the various heat-shrink synthetics. These range from the very lightweight material used to cover airplane wings to the heavier material sold by George Dyson. Heat-shrink material is attractive because it can be sewed up and then tightened simply by passing a hot clothes iron over it. The elaborate stretching and lacing procedures described in this chapter for canvas are not necessary. In addition, synthetic fibers do not undergo the extreme tightening and loosening cycles that canvas undergoes when it gets wet and then dries out again. Synthetics are also rot-resistant.

They're not ideal, though, despite these advantages. Heat-shrink fabrics have some drawbacks that have prevented me from using them on a wooden frame. In the first place, synthetics are more expensive than cotton. Although this is a consideration, it's not serious enough to disqualify them as a suitable covering for wooden boats.

More serious, in my view, is the strength mismatch between synthetics and the wooden frame. The heavier synthetics are a lot stronger than the lightweight wooden frame, which might get damaged during rough use.

To repair any kind of hull damage, you'll probably have to remove the skin. If the skin is canvas, that's a pretty simple task. You stretch it, lace it back up, sew it, and repaint the seams. But if the skin is heat-shrink synthetic you may run into trouble. Unless it has some shrink left in it, you may have a hard time getting it tight again, in which case you'll have to throw away the old skin and put on a new one.

If I were to use synthetic skin with a wooden frame, I'd go with the very lightweight skin and be careful not to damage it.

Choosing the Canvas

Choosing canvas is fortunately much easier than choosing your lumber. I have used both #10 and #8 cotton duck, the smaller number indicating a heavier canvas. The easier of the two to work with is naturally the lighter #10 canvas. The #8 canvas is almost like cardboard and is much more difficult to stretch tight, so I

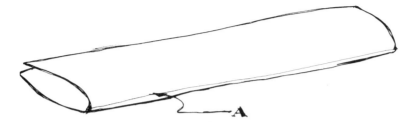

Figure 10-1. *Fold the canvas in half lengthwise and mark the centerline, A, with a crayon or a piece of drawing charcoal.*

recommend #10 canvas.

The canvas should be untreated cotton duck—don't buy anything that's already waterproofed. Get it in a 48-inch (120 cm) width, which is wide enough to wrap around the boat except in the vicinity of the cockpit, where you need to patch in a piece. The length of the canvas should equal the length of the boat, rounded up to the nearest foot, yard, or the smallest unit that your supplier will let you buy.

There's one thing to be aware of when you buy your canvas. When you stretch it to put it in the boat, you'll increase its length by at least 8 inches (20 cm). And remember to buy a yard or two extra if you want to experiment with sewing your own storage bags and other canvas gear.

Marking the Centerline

Fold the canvas in half lengthwise and run a soft pencil, crayon, or piece of charcoal along the crease to mark the centerline.

Fitting the Canvas

With your boat inverted on the sawhorses, drape the canvas over the boat and align the center of the canvas with the keelson. Trim the canvas to length so there are about 2 inches (5 cm) of over-

Figure 10-2. *Drape the canvas over the inverted boat and staple it to the keelson. Be careful not to staple into lashings.*

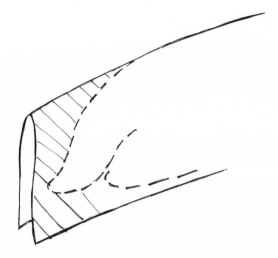

hang on either end of the boat. When you stretch the canvas along the length of the boat, you will get at least another 6 inches (15 cm) of overhang, so don't worry about trimming it too tight.

Before you can start sewing the bow, you need to trim some of the excess canvas in that area. Figure 10-3 shows what needs to be trimmed. Leave about ½ inch (13 mm) of overlap. Trim only a little ahead of where you are going to sew so you don't overtrim.

Sewing the Bow

Figure 10-4. Arrows indicate direction of sewing at the bow.

The sewing starts at the bow, at the very tip. Sew around the horn and into the jaw, trimming as you go along. There will be an opening at least part of the way. Stitch all the way to the end of the jaw to pull the canvas from both sides into the middle. Work your way back out of the jaw and stitch up toward the top of the bow plate. Stop when you get to the top of the bow plate. Figure 10-4 shows the direction of the sewing.

Figures 10-5 and 10-6 show some close-ups of the sewing on the bow.

Stretching the Canvas

Now that you have attached the canvas at the bow, you are ready to stretch the canvas longitudinally. You should do this on a dry day or in a dry room. The canvas has a tendency to shrink when the humidity is high.

Ideally, you can have somebody hang onto the boat while you stretch the canvas. The best way is for your partner to get under the boat, face the back, and hang on to one of the deck beams while you pull from the back. If you don't have a helper, brace one leg against a deck beam while you pull. The easiest way I have found to stretch the canvas is to grab hold of a double layer and pull it with a pair of pliers, preferably something like Vise-Grips. Pull back on the canvas with all your might. You should be able to stretch it beyond its starting point by at least 6 inches (15 cm). The maximum stretch is probably 9 inches (23 cm). When it is stretched as far as you can get it, make a mark where the canvas lines up with the end of the tailfin.

Release the canvas and sew the two halves together 1 inch (2.5 cm) forward of the mark for at least 4 inches (10 cm). Do the stretching again and hook the sewn corner of the canvas over the end of the tailfin. If you think you can stretch the

Figure 10-5. The bow seam starts at the bottom and goes up. The lumpy stuff at the bottom of the seam is ice.

Figure 10-6. View of bow stitching. Bad planning and excess trimming made a patch necessary at the tip of the bow plate.

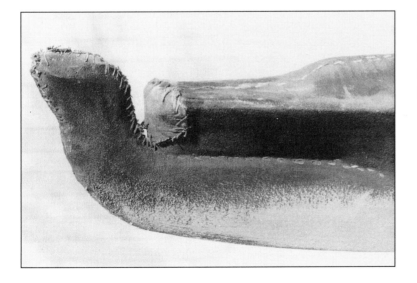

Figure 10-7. *While one person hangs on to the boat, the other person stretches the canvas longitudinally.*

canvas more, unhook it from the tailfin and resew it 1 inch or so (2.5 cm) farther forward.

Lacing the Deck

In addition to being stretched longitudinally, the canvas needs to be stretched around the hull. You'll do this by sewing loops into the canvas, lacing some cord through the loops, and tightening the cord as if it were laces on a pair of shoes.

While the deck is still upside down, staple the canvas to the keelson in about a dozen places, making sure it is centered. The staples will keep the canvas in place while you stretch it around the hull.

Turn the boat over and drape the canvas over the deck.

You're now ready to mark the position of the lacing loops on the canvas. The lacing will go from both ends of the boat to within a handspan of the cockpit. At the bow end, start marking about 18 inches (46 cm) back from the bow. Space the marks a handspan apart and about three fingers' width in from the edge of the gunwales. At the tail end, start marking about a handspan forward from the end of the gunwales.

Figure 10-8. *Fold the skin over the deck of the boat and put marks near the edge a handspan apart. The marks indicate where you will put the lacing loops.*

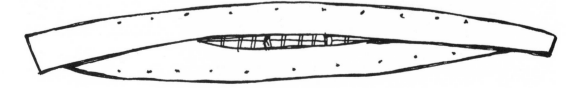

Sew a double loop at each dot with some strong twine. Size the loops by tying them around a ¼-inch (6 mm) dowel. Tie off the ends with a square knot.

Start at the bow and lace up the loops with some ⅛-inch line. Work your way toward the cockpit and tie off the ends in a knot that you can undo. Then start at the tail and work toward the cockpit. Tie those ends off too.

Don't tighten the laces too much on the first pass. You can pull the loops right out of the canvas if you're not careful. The best way to tighten the canvas is with two people. While one person grabs the flaps of overlapping canvas and pulls them toward the center, the other person takes the slack out of the lacing. Pulling on the canvas is more effective and safer than trying to tighten the canvas just by pulling on the lacing. After you have made your first pass at tightening, work back over the whole length of the boat and see if you can get any more slack out of it. If you have done a good job, your canvas should have a tight drum feel to it.

Figure 10-9. Tie lacing loops around a dowel.

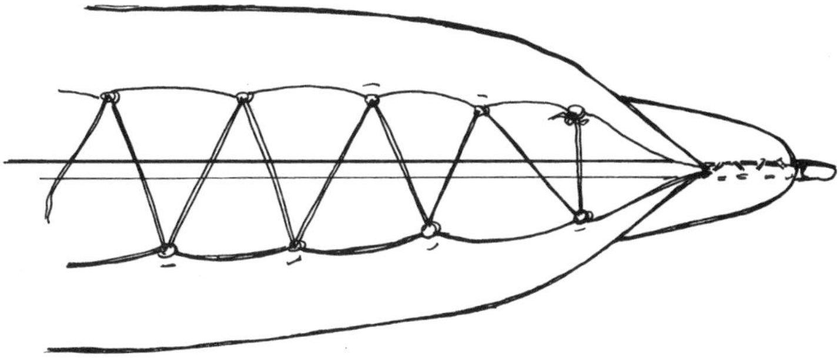

Figure 10-10. Lace up the deck to tighten the skin around the hull.

Trimming the Canvas

You should have excess canvas at both ends of the boat and not enough canvas near the cockpit. The idea is to trim off the excess near the end and use some of it to fill in the gaps.

Figure 10-11. Canvas should be trimmed to 2 inches (5 cm) of overlap.

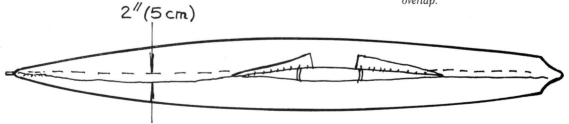

2″(5 cm)

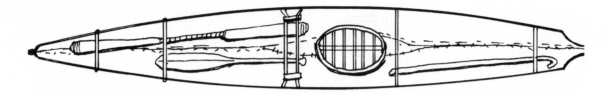

Figure 10-12. Deck straps should be positioned to allow storage of commonly carried objects such as paddles and fishing rods.

Overlap the canvas on the deck and trim it so you have 2 inches (5 cm) of overlap. This should leave you with four long, skinny, triangular pieces of canvas. Use two of them to fill in the gaps on either side of the cockpit. For now, all you will do is sew them to one of the edges of the canvas adjacent to the gap.

Planning the Deck Straps

As you sew up the deck, you drill holes through the skin and through the gunwales and pull the ends of the deck straps through these holes and tie them off on the inside. You want to sew past the point where the deck strap passes over the seam before attaching it, otherwise you will have to sew under the deck strap, which is a nuisance. Be careful, though, that you don't sew so far ahead that you can't reach inside the boat to tie off the ends of the deck straps.

Early pictures show that Aleut hunters used the deck straps to hold their darts, throwing boards, and bolas. Deck straps were spaced according to the length of the darts. I space my deck straps to hold spare paddles. Deck straps should be loose enough so you can get a paddle under them but not so loose that waves coming over the deck will wash the paddle away. I like leather straps for my decks because they lie flat. If you use rope, go with a ¼-inch (6 mm) diameter.

Don't overdo things in this department. An excessive amount of strapping on a seagoing boat is a waste of time at best and dangerous at worst. For one thing, anything strapped to your deck will act as a sail in a crosswind and will tend to pull the boat upwind or downwind if you don't have the same amount of sail fore and aft. If you happen to get into bad weather and breaking waves, the waves will want to wash the gear off your deck. You will then become preoccupied with saving your gear and forget about paddling, possibly inviting capsize. If you have to launch or land in surf, anything just tucked under deck straps and not tied down

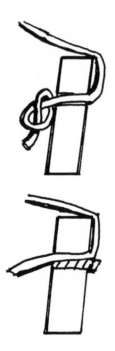

Figure 10-13. Deck straps can be tied off on the inside of the gunwales (top) or fixed with a wooden peg if added after the deck has been closed off.

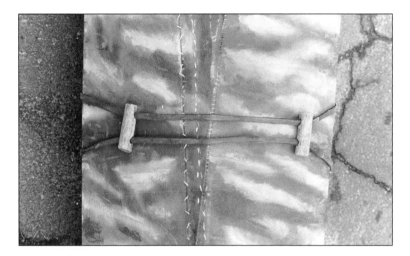

Figure 10-14. *Deck straps forward of the cockpit with tighteners. Straps are tightened by sliding the toggles toward the gunwales.*

Figure 10-15. *An example of a boat with too much gear on the deck. The problem was that the weather was too warm and I had to stow clothes that I was expecting to wear. This caused overflow of other items onto the deck.*

will most likely be washed away.

Anything lashed will still tend to wash off and dangle at the end of its rope, waiting to tangle your paddle and endanger you if you capsize. So keep the strapping simple and your deck load to a minimum.

Sewing the Deck Seam

There's more than one way to do the deck seam. Two methods I've used are a lap seam and a rolled seam. In the lap seam, you simply overlap the two flaps of skin by about an inch and, using two needles, sew back and forth as if you were lacing a pair of shoes. This is probably the simplest way to go. The stitching pattern is shown in Figure 10-16.

The other way to sew the seam is more elaborate and time-consuming but looks neater when done. This method is covered in more detail below.

Sewing the First Seam

To close the hull of the boat, you will need to sew the two edges of the skin together along the

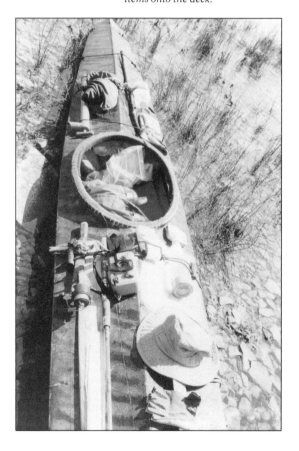

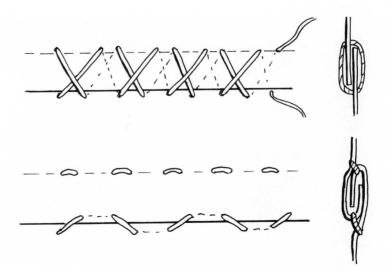

Figure 10-16. Diagram of a lap seam (top) and a folded seam (bottom). A cross section of both seams is shown on the right. The lap seam is simpler to sew but looks more ragged because it leaves a cut edge exposed.

Figure 10-17. Diagram of the first seam. The stitching simply goes back and forth.

ridge line of the boat. You'll need to sew one seam first, trim the excess skin to leave about a 2-inch (5 cm) flap, fold that flap over, and then sew it down on the deck with a second seam.

Starting at the bow, match the two flaps of skin face to face and sew them as shown below. Work toward the cockpit and stop when you are a few inches past the cockpit rim. Start the stitches far enough from the seam so that as you tighten up the string, you pull the skin flaps toward the middle, leaving about a ⅛-inch (3 mm) gap between them. If the two flaps are touching, you probably aren't pulling all the slack out of the skin.

When you sew the seam on the back deck, start at the bottom of the tailpiece and work up and toward the cockpit. The Aleuts sewed the bottommost part of the skin at the tail into a tube. They tied this tube off when the boat was in use and untied it to drain water out of the boat when it was pulled up on the beach. The tube could also be used as a place to tie a rudder. See Appendix 4 on sails and rudders for details.

In my experience, the tube is very slow in draining water out of the boat, but fast in leaking water into the boat if it isn't sealed and tied off properly. I don't recommend its use unless you want it for attaching a rudder.

Opposite Page: Figure 10-18. Sewing the first seam.

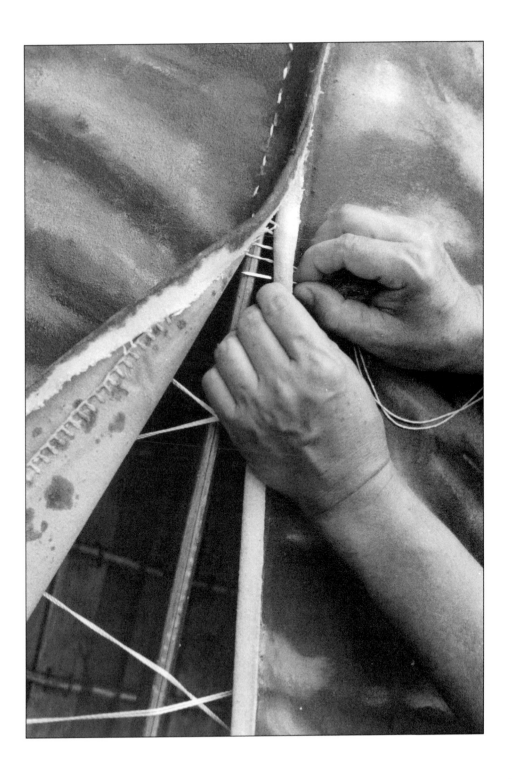

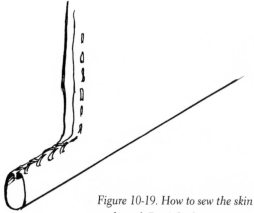

Figure 10-19. *How to sew the skin at the tail. Don't bother putting on a drain tube unless you want to attach a rudder.*

Figure 10-20. *The tube in the tail is tied to prevent leakage of water into the boat.*

Sewing the Second Seam

Before you start the second seam, trim the flaps of skin at the edge of the first seam so that one is about 1 inch (2.5 cm) wider than the other.

Fold the flaps of skin over so the wider of the two lies over the narrower, then tuck the wider under the narrower.

Using a curved needle, sew first through the deck, then through the top layer of the overlapped skin, then back through the deck and so on.

Sewing Around the Cockpit Coaming

To keep the sprayskirt attached to the cockpit coaming, the skin needs to be pulled up at the bottom of the coaming. To accom-

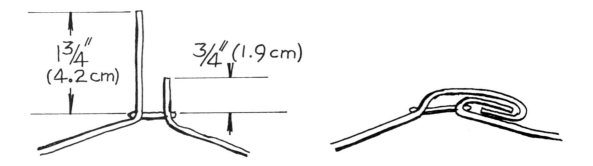

plish this, drill a set of holes in the coaming about ½ inch (13 mm) from the bottom and 2 inches (5 cm) apart. Sew from the inside through the hole and the skin, then back through the skin and into the same hole you sewed out of.

Next, fold the skin over the coaming and down into the cockpit. If need be, cut slits in the canvas inside the cockpit so you can fold it down. Sew the flaps down. You can anchor your stitches to the stitching already on the inside of the coaming.

Figure 10-21. After you have sewed the first seam, trim the canvas along the seam so one side is wider than the other. Fold the longer side over and under as shown on the right.

Attaching a Coaming Rim

Aleuts used to put a rim on the coaming before covering the coaming with skin but, in my experience, canvas sewed over the

Figure 10-22. Use the curved needle to sew the second seam. Alternate between sewing through the flap and through the skin of the deck. Don't attempt to sew through both the flap and the deck at the same time.

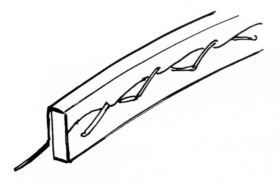

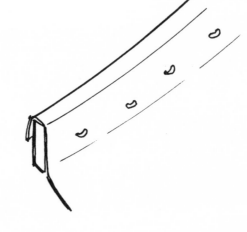

Figure 10-23. The traditional Bering Strait sewing pattern. The inside view is on the left and the outside view is on the right.

rim does not create enough of a lip. It lets the sprayskirt pull off in rough water. I've lately switched to sewing on the rim after sewing the skin around the coaming. I've not since had any trouble with the sprayskirt pulling off.

Painting the Skin

Whatever type of paint you use for the canvas, it needs to waterproof the canvas and fill the weave to give you a smooth hull. If you don't use enough paint, the boat's skin will be rough, which

Figure 10-24. This pattern shows the skin pulled over the top of the coaming and attached to stitching that goes through the coaming.

will produce drag and make the boat slow. If you use too much paint, your boat will gain a lot of weight and the thicker paint will crack sooner. I usually compromise by putting two coats on the deck and three coats on the bottom of the hull. This way I can have a smooth finish on the bottom where it's needed and light weight on the top where a smooth finish isn't needed.

I've used Thompson's Water Seal as the first coat on most of my boats. I paint it on straight out of the can. I suspect that the water seal has a mildew retardant in it since the treated canvas does not develop mildew spots as untreated canvas does. The only drawback of the Water Seal is that it takes several days to dry before you can paint over it with oil paints, and several weeks before you can paint over it with latex-based paints.

I have some friends who have used thinned oil paint for the first coat, and they tell me that if soaked into the canvas this also prevents mildew.

Aircraft dope shrinks and tightens the skin when it dries. This is a nice feature, but aircraft dope is hard to come by and most likely more expensive than oil paint.

I've used both oil-based paint and a latex-based rubberized roof paint. The roof paint works pretty well but only comes in black and white. If you are interested in other colors, go with the oil paint. The roof paint can be used as is and needs to be put on in sufficient coats to fill the weave of the canvas.

Oil paint needs to be put on in stages. If you haven't treated the canvas with a water seal product, mix white exterior oil-based primer, linseed oil, and turpentine in a 2, 2, 1 ratio for the first coat. If you have used the water seal, use the oil-based primer straight out of the can. When the oil paint has dried to a pudding-like consistency, rub the palm of your hand over the hull to push the paint down into the weave. This will give you smooth paint a lot faster than if you just paint successive coats. Once the paint is dry, lightly sand the hull and paint it again. Quit when the hull is smooth.

For a finish coat, I mix linseed oil with some artist's oil paint out of the tube to a fairly translucent consistency and either paint it on if I want a design or rub it on with a rag if I want a single color coat. The advantage of this technique is that it gives you color without adding a lot of weight to the boat. If you don't like mixing your own color paint, get some colored house paint. Don't use high gloss enamel paints since these dry very hard and crack easily.

If you have put a drain tube on the tail of the boat, be sure to paint that, too, or it will be a place where water seeps into your boat on long trips. Also be sure to paint the skin all the way to the top of the cockpit rim and at least a little way into the inside of the cockpit. I used to leave off the paint here and found that water

Figure 10-26. A wooden rub strip prevents the skin from wearing through at the tail end of the boat.

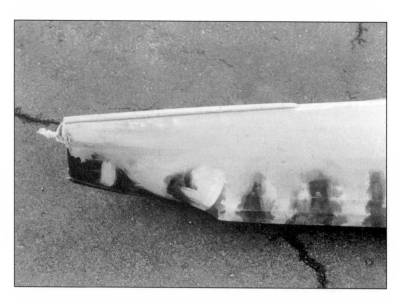

drips off the cockpit rim and rots the canvas when the boat is stored upside down outdoors.

Installing a Rub Strip

Because the Aleuts replaced the skin on their boats every year or two, the skin never wore enough to warrant rub strips. In your case, however, the skin will last five years or more, and during this time you'll get enough wear at the tail end of the keelson to warrant some kind of rub strip. Two options for rub strips are available to you. The first is made from a strip of wood and is inspired by the Greenland kayaks. The second is just an extra layer or two of canvas glued to the skin in the tail area.

To make a wooden rub strip, cut a strip of hardwood ¾ inch (1.9 cm) wide and 3 feet (91 cm) long. Drill and peg it to the tail end of the keelson. Use some epoxy or waterproof glue when you put in the pegs. This should help to minimize leakage where the pegs pierce the skin.

To make a canvas rub strip, cut a strip of canvas 1½ inches (3.8 cm) wide and 3 feet (91 cm) long. Glue this to the tail end of the keelson using latex roofing paint. Glue another 6-inch (15 cm) long strip near the very tail for extra reinforcement.

11 Kayak Dress

You won't need your yachting cap and blazer when you go kayaking. The emphasis in kayak dress is on survival. Comfort and looks are secondary, especially in cold water.

If you are lucky enough to paddle warm water, some of this chapter will be irrelevant, but you'll still need a sprayskirt—and you may want to make yourself a paddle jacket.

Yes, you can make a jacket. Once you've sewn the skin onto your boat, you'll have the necessary skill and confidence to make many of your own kayak clothing accessories. A sewing machine helps a lot, of course. I bought a new one in 1989 for $99 and it paid for itself in no time with the savings on a sprayskirt, a paddle jacket, and several dry bags.

Figure 11-1. When you're paddling in cold weather, you need to protect yourself with warm, waterproof clothing. (Martin Honel photo)

The Sprayskirt

You'll need a sprayskirt to keep water from getting into the cockpit. Most sprayskirts you can buy are too big to fit your cockpit, so I'll tell you how to make your own.

Patterns for sprayskirts are shown in Figures 11-2 and 11-3. The bottom of the skirt must match the outside diameter of the coaming rim. Allow maybe 3 inches (8 cm) for shrinkage; even nylon shrinks a little. Allow more for cotton. Remember that 3 extra inches in circumference equals only about 1 inch (2.5 cm) in diameter, which comes out to about ½ inch (13 mm) extra on each side. However, don't go too far oversize on the diameter of the skirt. The wrinkles caused by cinching in the excess material will allow water to seep into the cockpit when you are doing rolls or other underwater maneuvers.

Sew a grab loop to the front of the sprayskirt. The grab loop lets you pull the sprayskirt free from the cockpit coaming if you should capsize and need to do a wet exit. The grab loop should be big enough so you can pull it even if you are wearing gloves. You can make your sprayskirt from waterproofed nylon or you can make it from cotton, which you waterproof with a mixture of boiled linseed oil and beeswax.

The Paddling Jacket

Aleutian kayakers used to wear waterproof, gut-skin parkas that looked like hooded, below-the-knee raincoats. They wore the

(Left) Figure 11-2. The top of the sprayskirt should be made to fit your chest. The bottom should be made to fit the cockpit. Suspenders hold up the top and can be used to keep water from puddling in your lap. The grab loop in front lets you pull the skirt free of the cockpit when you need to exit.

(Right) Figure 11-3. An alternate two-piece sprayskirt design that is useful for larger cockpits.

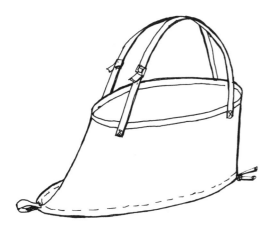

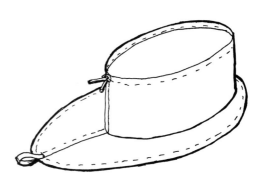

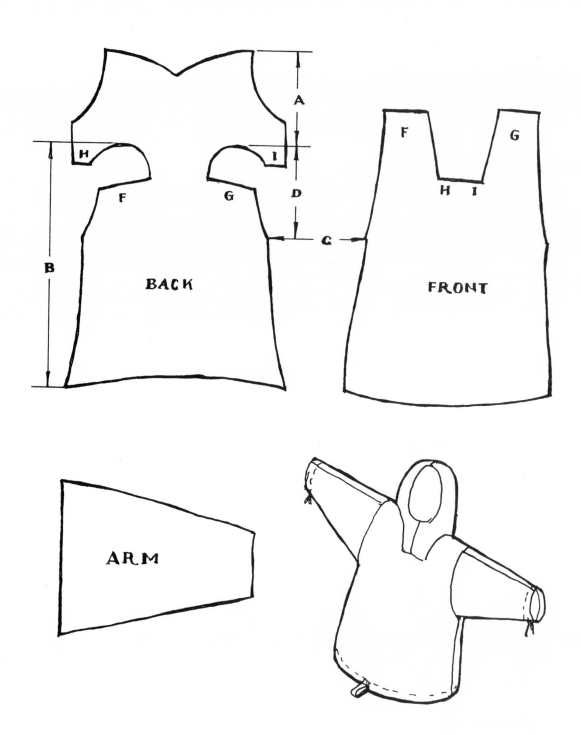

parkas along with the sprayskirts to seal themselves into their boats. You can take a similar approach or you can size the bottom hem of your paddling jacket to fit the cockpit. Your paddling jacket will then be a sprayskirt as well. The paddling jacket/sprayskirt combination is a Greenland invention. But unless you are a purist, I think the dual-purpose jacket is more convenient and more waterproof.

If you paddle primarily in warm or hot weather, the paddling jacket will be too hot and you ought to stick with the sprayskirt. A waterproof paddling jacket served the same function for the traditional paddler as the drysuit serves for the modern recreational paddler.

The pattern for the paddling jacket is shown in Figure 11-4. Minimum length is just above the knee. You need the length if you're going to do rolls. If the jacket is too short and you lean back, you'll pull the hem of the skirt right off the coaming. Fit in the body should be loose so you can wear a winter jacket and your life vest under the paddling jacket.

Watch the dimensions of the hood. The fit should be snug so you can make it waterproof, but leave enough room so you can wear a diving hood or some kind of hat under the hood in cold weather. Don't make the hood too small or you'll end up supporting the weight of the jacket on your head instead of on your shoulders. This is especially important if you get a wave in your lap. Its weight will be pulling down on the paddling jacket.

You can seal the seams from the outside with a product called Aquaseal, which is neoprene in solution. When it's dry it's very tough. It takes 12 hours or so to cure but it's well worth the bother. Aquaseal is sold in dive shops.

Life Vest

The Coast Guard calls this item of kayak dress a "personal flotation device," or PFD. Don't try to make one of these—buy one. The fit is important. If it's too loose, it'll slide up when you're in the water and you'll have a hard time breathing because the front of the vest will cover your mouth. You'll also have a hard time hearing because the sides of the vest will be around your ears.

If the vest is too tight, you'll have a hard time breathing because you can't expand your chest. If you paddle in cold

(Opposite Page) Figure 11-4. This traditional pattern for a paddling jacket economizes on seams to minimize water leakage. A is the distance from the top of your head to the top of your shoulders. B is the distance from the top of your shoulders to just above your knees. C is the bottom of the armhole. D is the distance from the top of the shoulder to the bottom of the armhole. Points marked F, G, H, and I on the back match corresponding points on the front.

weather, make sure the PFD will fit over your jacket or layers of cold weather wear.

Dressing for the Cold

The rule when paddling is to dress for the temperature of the water, not the air. This means that if the air temperature is 80°F(25°C) and the water is 50°F (10°C) you need to wear a wetsuit or several layers of clothes and a drysuit.

Wearing proper clothing when paddling is essential to your survival as a paddler. I say this as a paddler who mostly goes paddling on Lake Michigan, which, for 10 months of the year, is too cold for swimming. The good news about water is that no matter how cold the air, water will not get much colder than its freezing point of 32°F (0°C) for fresh water. If you paddle in water that cold, you should dress so you can survive long enough to swim ashore. I have found that a drysuit with three layers of clothes will do the trick.

For the first layer, I wear expedition weight polyester longjohns and a long-sleeve top. Over that I wear polyester pile sweatpants and a polyester pile sweater on top. For the third layer, I wear a polyester pile vest a size larger than the sweater. It's important to keep your clothes from bunching up under your armpits or they will start chafing.

Figure 11-5. For cold weather and cold water paddling, warm gloves, boots, and a hood are essential.

On my feet, I wear neoprene socks or boots. On my head, I wear a neoprene diving hood. On my hands, I wear neoprene diving gloves. Generally, dive shops have better headgear and gloves for cold weather than do kayak shops.

If you don't want to wear clothes made from synthetic fibers, you can go with wool. You may have to go to an Army surplus store to get some items such as wool pants. I still recommend a drysuit, however.

12 Accessories

There's certainly no shortage of accessories that you could fit to your kayak if you wanted to, and could afford to. Some of them are sold more for commercial reasons than practical reasons, though, so let's take a critical look at some of the more useful items such as seat cushions, dry bags, airbags, boathooks, and more.

Airbags

When I'm playing in surf where there is a good chance of the boat filling with water, I always have at least one airbag in the boat; two are preferable.

A kayak without airbags will float a little, but it will have so much water in it that it will be hard to move. The kayak will also be susceptible to damage should it ram into the beach with a full load of water. If you're paddling with someone else and you should exit the boat and swamp it, without airbags the boat will be

Figure 12-1. Flotation bags will reduce the amount of water that gets into your boat if you have to exit. Having one bag in back and one in front is best.

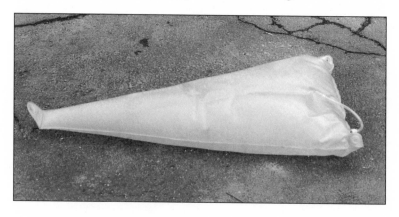

so heavy you will find it nearly impossible to empty unless you've had lots of practice. Airbags are available at kayak stores.

Dry Bags

If you are camping and carrying a load, your dry bags will have to provide flotation for your boat. If your dry bags aren't really dry, line them with plastic garbage bags to make them so.

Commercial dry bags, except for the very smallest, will not fit into an Aleut kayak. You are better off making your own bags out of canvas and waterproofing them. You can also make them out of waterproofed material such as coated nylon.

Canvas is an attractive material to use since there is usually some left over after skinning a boat. Canvas bags are also stiff, which makes them easier to shove into remote regions of the kayak. However, canvas is bulkier than nylon, making nylon more attractive if space is at an absolute premium.

The best time to fit the bags is before you put the skin on the boat. I size the bags so one fits in back of the cockpit and two fit in front of the cockpit. I make the bags a little longer than necessary so I can put grommets in the edge and cinch them up with a rope. This sort of closure is not waterproof, so you need to line the inside of the bag with plastic garbage bags. If you want the bag to be waterproof, try a rolled seam closure instead of grommets.

Figure 12-2. Dry bags can be made from canvas or treated nylon. Fit them to your boat before you put the skin on.

The main problem with dry bags is that as you stuff them, they assume a circular cross section while the space inside your kayak is elliptical. If this is a problem, you may want to go to a two-bag, side-by-side packing scheme instead of the single large bag.

Seat Cushion

Commercial kayaks usually have some kind of seat. Do not put a seat in your kayak. Line the bottom of the cockpit area with an inexpensive foam camping mat doubled or tripled. An actual seat would raise your center of gravity too much and make the boat unstable.

Bilge Pump

Figure 12-3. A pump is handy for getting water out of the bottom of your boat when you're underway. But a pump like this is not useful for emptying a completely swamped boat.

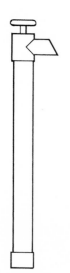

I've never had to use a pump to empty a kayak after a capsize and I hope I never will. Pumping out a swamped baidarka, even if it has flotation, could take half an hour. A pump takes two hands to operate so it's useless in rough water unless you can stabilize your boat by rigging your paddle as an outrigger. If you travel in a group, you can get a partner to hold on to your boat while you pump.

The other problem with a pump is that you need to open the sprayskirt to stick the end of the pump into the boat. You had better pump faster than new water comes into the cockpit. I think a pump is mainly useful for getting residual water out of the boat after a team effort has turned the swamped boat upside down to get most of the water out. As with all rescue equipment, you'd better give your pump a good trial before counting on it to get you out of a jam.

Those intrepid Aleuts used to carry hollow wooden tubes, with which they sucked water out of their boats. I suspect that these tubes were used as bilge pumps to clear seepage out of the bottom of the boat. I don't think they were practical instruments for emptying a swamped boat.

Rescue and Towing Ropes

I own a rescue rope but haven't had occasion to use it. People who take inexperienced kayakers out on trips use them to tow slow paddlers on the way back. I suppose you could tow a disabled paddler if you had a rope. However, this is one of those maneuvers that you need to practice under calm conditions to have any chance of its working when you really need it.

The biggest danger of stray rope is that you'll capsize and get tangled in it, preventing you from rolling, and forcing you to exit the boat.

Deck Knife

If you carry a rescue rope, you should also carry a deck knife so you can cut the rope if you get tangled in it.

The other purpose of a knife is to cut a hole in the boat to let the water drain out. I once got blown into some rocks and didn't have enough energy to get off them. As soon as I stepped out of the boat, waves filled it with water. Since I was standing in water up to my hips, I couldn't manage to drain the boat. With all the water in it, it was too heavy for me to lift up on the rocks.

Someone on shore had seen me and called the fire department. When they came, I got them to haul the boat up the rocks for me. If I'd had a knife, I could have cut a hole near the bow to let the water drain out and gotten the boat up on the rocks by myself. Of course, now I stay away from the rocks when the surf is up. And I still don't carry a deck knife.

Boathook

A 4- or 5-foot (122 cm or 152 cm) stick with some sort of hook on the end is handy for fishing dry bags out of the boat when unloading and pushing them back in when loading. When you are underway, you can stow the boathook on deck, under the deck lines.

Compass

I own a compass, but I've always done line-of-sight navigation. The compass comes in handy when you cannot see your destination because it is obscured by fog or is beyond the horizon. There are a number of books on kayak navigation. You should refer to one of them if you intend to paddle beyond the horizon.

Assorted Emergency Gear

If you go on longer trips where you'll be some miles from land, you may want to take some emergency gear such as flares, smoke, marker dye, and a marine-band VHF radio. Your best bet, though, is to stay off the water when conditions are so rough that you need to use the distress gear.

The type of emergency gear you take depends a lot on where you paddle. If you operate near busy shipping lanes, signaling devices or a radio can bring help in a hurry. But if you paddle remote areas, the chances are that no one will be around to see or hear your signals.

(Opposite Page) Figure 12-4. A boathook is useful for fishing bags out of your kayak and jamming them back in.

13 Using Your Boat

The proof of your boat is in the paddling. When your boat is finished, wait for a pleasant day and take it to a nice, friendly body of water. Don't start off in nasty water.

If you have never paddled before and your boat feels a little tippy, don't worry, this feeling will disappear as you get used to the boat. This may take a few outings, but you will get better and feel more comfortable.

With experience, you'll learn that a tippy boat is inherently more seaworthy than an overly stable one. But there's another reason for preferring a tippy boat to start with. When you're a beginner, a boat that dumps you once or twice will give you a proper respect for the water. People who get in trouble on the water are often beginners who, because they have very stable boats, can get out on water for which their skills are no match. As the weather changes for the worse or their strength wanes, they find themselves capsized and looking at a long swim. Without proper thermal insulation, this can mean hypothermia and possibly death.

Paddling Skills

If you have never kayaked before, try to get some lessons in rolling and other self-rescue techniques before you venture out on your own. Classes are available at sea-kayaking symposiums.

Most large cities near a body of water will have a kayaking club or other kayakers willing to help you learn. There is plenty of information in kayaking books and magazines on how to paddle. However, just in case you don't have ready access to any of these, I'll cover a few of the basics.

Going on the Water

Don't step into a kayak unless you are prepared to get wet. It's certainly possible to paddle a kayak without getting wet, but don't count on it, especially when you are first starting out. This means that if you don't have a drysuit or wetsuit and you wouldn't feel comfortable swimming back to shore, stay off the water.

Getting into Your Kayak

On a lot of commercial kayaks with large cockpits, you can just step into the cockpit and sit down. Getting into your Aleut kayak is a little more complicated. The instructions I offer here are intended for sandy beaches. Once you've mastered this technique, you can create your own launching techniques for difficult situations.

The first step in launching is to position your boat with its bow in the water and the cockpit at the edge of the water. Next you straddle the boat and sit down on the deck just behind the cockpit. Position your paddle behind you so you are sitting on one blade with the rest of the paddle extended outward from the boat at a right angle. The paddle will act as an outrigger and stabilize you while you get into the boat.

Next, you need to swish your feet back and forth in the water to get the dirt off. Any dirt you bring into the boat will get between the frame and the skin and abrade both of them. This is important etiquette for a skin boater and something you will also need to teach friends with plastic boats if they want to try your boat.

Once your feet are clean, lift them into the boat while leaning toward the side on which your paddle is extended. Failure to lean correctly can leave you flopped over on your side. Straighten your legs, and wiggle forward until your rear clears the back of the cockpit. Now lower yourself to the floor of the boat.

All this time, both hands stay on your paddle. If you take your hands off the paddle you may well find it swept out of reach

Figure 13-1. To get into your kayak, slide forward with your legs straight.

Figure 13-2. Once you are in your kayak and the sprayskirt is sealed, you are ready to push yourself into the water, or in this case, slide into the water off the ice.

by an incoming wave. You will then have to get out of the boat and start all over again.

Before you do anything else, bring the paddle around and rest it on the coaming just in front of you. This will minimize the chance of incoming surf washing your paddle away from you. Now tighten the sprayskirt around the cockpit coaming. When the sprayskirt is tight, grab the paddle in your preferred hand and get yourself the rest of the way into the water as best you can. Technique varies depending on conditions. Launching in surf is always more tricky because the edge of the water moves around.

Getting out of Your Kayak

To get out of your kayak, paddle as far up the beach as you can. You may have to wait until some of the bigger waves have pushed you up good and high before you try to exit. When you think you are as well-positioned as possible, undo the sprayskirt and place your paddle behind you, outrigger style. With your hands behind

you and on your paddle, push yourself up and wiggle out of the cockpit. This part is usually harder than getting in.

If there is surf, you will often get hit by a wave just as you are about halfway out of the boat. When you step out of the boat, step to the side closest to the water. Incoming surf will slam the boat into your legs if you get out on the wrong side. Drag or carry your boat and paddle out of reach of the waves.

The Wet Exit

If you've never paddled before, take a friend along on your first outing. Your friend will stand by you while you do a wet exit.

Get into your boat, fasten the sprayskirt, and paddle into thigh-deep water. When your friend has waded out and is standing next to you, capsize the boat and get out of it.

There are several things to keep in mind when you do this. First, you might want to wear nose plugs when doing a wet exit. This will minimize the discomfort. Second, since the first thing you'll have to do when you are upside down is pull the sprayskirt loose from the cockpit coaming, you might want to practice this on dry land with one hand and your eyes closed. Don't be scared. Getting out of your kayak when it is upside down is a lot easier than either getting into or out of it when it is right side up. When you are hanging in your kayak upside down, gravity is helping you and sliding out of your kayak is natural. When you do a wet exit, hang on to your paddle.

Before you attempt your wet exit, tell your friend that if you slap the hull of the boat with the flat of your hand three times, this means you would like him to grab your arm and pull you up. When you are ready, capsize the boat while holding the paddle at your side. When you are upside down, seize the grab loop at the front of the sprayskirt and pull out and up. Then put a hand on either side of the cockpit and push yourself free. Stand up and push your boat back to the beach. You have mastered the wet exit and know that if your boat capsizes, you will not be trapped in it.

Bracing

An important part of paddling a boat is bracing. Bracing gives your boat stability. When you have your paddle in the water, you can increase the effective width of your boat from 21 inches (53 cm) to 48 inches (122 cm) just by leaning on your paddle. When you are resting, put the flat of the paddle blade across the cockpit with the other end of the blade sticking out at a right angle. If you lean, lean to the side on which your paddle is extended. This is one of the reasons both blades of your paddle should be in the same plane and not feathered as most commercial paddles are.

When you paddle, you will also need to brace. Bracing while paddling is nothing more than leaning toward the side on which the paddle is extended. You will get the hang of this in no time. Be aware, however, that too much lean will put you over on your side.

Survival

Kayaking in cold water is a potentially deadly undertaking even if you paddle in a group. Your best line of defense is not to be on the water when conditions require any kind of survival skills. Of course, unless you are familiar with the weather and water conditions in the area where you paddle, you may not recognize dangerous conditions and know enough to stay off the water. If you are new to an area, get as much information about the water as you can. Talk to other paddlers, find out about currents, listen to weather reports, and so on.

Know your own limits. Practice paddling in wind and waves under controlled conditions where you can pull into shore when conditions become too much for you. A long weekend outing or a vacation trip is not the time to test your limits.

Your second-best line of defense is a drysuit with several layers of pile clothes underneath. A good drysuit with sufficient layers will allow you to stay in the water for at least half an hour without ill effects. If you paddle near shore, a drysuit will allow you to swim your boat back to shore if you can't get back in it. I have done this on more than one occasion and can attest to its efficacy.

Group rescues require that you spend some time in the water while someone drags your boat across their boat to get the water out of it. By the time this is done and you get back in the boat, you may not be capable of paddling any longer if you aren't wearing a drysuit. You are then endangering your partners.

Your best bet for continuing to enjoy the sport is to exercise good judgment. Where most people seem to get themselves in trouble is long crossings of open water. The water may be perfectly fine when they start but become nasty before they reach their destination.

Even the original kayakers died in large numbers while kayaking. I believe they did so because they had to be out on the water in pursuit of game. Sooner or later they would get caught in bad weather that they could not survive. I don't think that kayaking has to be as dangerous for modern recreational kayakers. You can stay off the water when it gets nasty. You can also avoid long crossings until you've gotten a weather forecast that assures you of benign conditions.

Rescue Methods

Rescue methods are designed to get you into a safe position after your boat has turned upside down. Don't ever rely on any rescue method that you haven't practiced under the conditions in which you'll actually need it. Don't count on something that worked in a calm swimming pool to work in cold water with breaking waves and a 30-m.p.h. wind.

If you expect to paddle cold water and rough weather, practice your rescues in cold water and rough weather. If you are counting on group rescues, practice them with your friends in cold water and rough weather. If your friends don't want to practice under these conditions, don't go paddling with them in cold water and rough weather.

Self Rescue

The best method of rescue is self rescue. If you paddle alone, it is the only method. The best method of self rescue is the roll. It is a good method because it is fast and expends little energy. In really rough water, any other kind of self rescue is ineffective. Once you get out of your boat, getting back in and bailing the water out uses up a tremendous amount of energy.

If the weather is so rough that it knocked you over once, it will probably knock you over again, especially after you used up all your energy getting back in the boat and pumping it out.

Figure 13-3. If you are wearing the right gear, doing rolls even in cold water is not a problem.

Rolling

The easiest way to learn rolling is to have someone else show you how. Once you have learned one roll, you can practice that roll until you are very good at it. You will then find other rolls easier to learn because if you do blow a new roll, you can get up with your old roll.

Some people simply can't learn how to roll. If you are one of these, concentrate on other self-rescue techniques and group rescues. You can find out about these methods in kayak how-to books.

Figure 13-4. You can get a considerable amount of gear into a kayak.

Figure 13-5. Whatever you can't get into the kayak ends up on the deck. Anything on the deck is likely to be washed off unless it is tied down. In this case, gear that should have been in the boat ended up on deck, displaced by clothes too warm to wear.

Group Rescue

Group rescue is intrinsically less reliable than self rescue because it requires at least two people. The rescue will only be as reliable as the least reliable person in the group. Group rescues are a favorite of tour guides because they are the only way to get inexperienced people back into a boat.

Cruising

Your Aleut kayak is a very good cruising boat. If you pack carefully, you can get a week's worth of food into it. If you pack dried food, you can probably get two weeks' worth of food in. If you pack low-bulk, backpacking-type gear, you can probably get three weeks' worth of food in.

1
APPENDIX

Fixups and Repairs

Got a problem? This appendix probably describes some ways to deal with it. The problems touched on here are ones you might encounter in building as well as ones you might run into after the boat is finished.

First let me repeat the obvious way of avoiding problems: Treat your boat well and it will treat you well. If you don't maintain your boat properly, it will remind you of your neglect. If you do your maintenance faithfully, your boat will respond in kind.

Figure 1. If your stringers break, you can splint and lash them.

Figure 2 (opposite page). If broken parts are inaccessible, you may need to slit the deck seam to get at them.

Broken Ribs and Stringers

If you break a rib or stringer on a finished boat and the break is accessible, carve a splint to bridge the break and lash it to the broken part.

If you break a rib or stringer in a place where you can't get at it, slit the deck seam to get access. Peel back the skin, unlash the affected part, replace it or splint it, and replace and resew the skin.

Paint Maintenance

If the canvas has been exposed, simply spot-paint it. Resist the temptation to give your boat a whole new coat of paint every so often. Not only will this add pounds to the weight of your boat, it will also accelerate the tendency of the paint to crack. If you have used oil paint on the skin and the paint has developed some hairline cracks, apply a thin coat of boiled linseed oil with a rag. Repeat if necessary. The linseed oil will fill the cracks in the skin.

Skin Repair

You can apply a patch to a small hole in the skin. Cut a canvas patch and glue it on with whatever works for you. I have found latex roofing paint to be very effective. After the patch dries, paint it to match the surrounding area.

If the skin tears, you need to mend it. Use a curved needle and cotton twine and sew in the pattern shown in Figure 3. If there's a gap, weave some twine back and forth between the stitches to fill in the gap. When you're done, fill the gaps with paint or with latex roofing paint. Don't worry about looks. The repair will give your boat more character.

Figure 3. Close tears in the skin by sewing (left), then weave the thread along the tear (right), to further strengthen the repair. Finish up by painting the repair to make it watertight. If the tear is big, you may want to glue a patch over it after you have done the sewing.

Wrongly Sized Parts

If a deck beam is too low and there's a gap between it and the deck stringer, fill the gap with a small wooden block or shim. Lashings will keep the shim in place. The same goes for gaps between ribs and stringers. Shim if you don't feel like redoing a rib.

If a deck beam is too high and you're afraid of weakening it by removing too much wood, cut a notch in the deck stringer to compensate for the extra elevation.

With wood being plentiful and relatively cheap, there isn't much virtue in salvaging a messed up part. I think it's more a matter of losing momentum when you stop to redo a part. A quick fix will keep you moving toward your goal and minimize the likelihood that you'll give up because you aren't making any progress.

Holes in the Wood

If you drilled a hole in the wrong place, where it's visible, and you don't like its looks, select or carve a matching dowel, put a little glue on it, and plug the hole. Trim the ends flush with the piece.

What to Do if Your Boat Doesn't Fit You

If you check your boat against the size of your body before you commit to building it a certain size, you shouldn't have any trouble fitting it. However, you can unintentionally make a boat too tight. I have done this more than once.

If that happens to you, don't despair. You can always do some disassembly and reassembly of a boat to make it fit better. Compare this to the experience of a friend of mine who built a kayak using glued wood construction. When he was done, he found the boat too tight for his feet and sold it for little more than the cost of materials. Skin-on-frame kayaks are more forgiving and you can always do some rearranging of parts to make a boat with marginal fit into a boat with good fit.

On one baidarka I made, the space between the knee brace and the ribs was too small for my legs. I could squeeze into the space if I was wearing shorts, but fitting with long pants was out of the question. I solved the problem by carving ½ inch out of the underside of the deck beam.

The first boat I ever built was a Greenland kayak. After

paddling it for over a year, I finally concluded that the cockpit was too far forward for my size. The bow was riding too low and the tail was sticking up too high. Every time the wind blew, the boat would want to turn into the wind. The boat was also a little tight to get into because the knee brace was too low.

In the meantime, I had built some baidarkas and could pull the Greenland kayak into drydock without losing any paddling time. I cut all the lashings that held the cockpit coaming to the skin. I opened the deck seam so I could get at the junction of the deck beam and the gunwales on either side of the cockpit. I sawed off the back brace and put a new one in place 3 inches behind the old one. I left the old knee brace in place and just added another one, 3 inches behind it. I made the new knee brace taller as well, so getting in and out of the boat would be easier. Then I sewed up the deck seam. I had to trim the skin at the back and patch in more skin in front of the cockpit. Then I replaced the coaming and repainted the seam and the new canvas.

Among other things, the boat had too much rocker, which I hadn't fixed. But now the tail sat a little lower and the bow rose much better into oncoming waves. So it is possible to open up a skin boat and rearrange its parts.

Steamboxes and Ribs

APPENDIX

If you should happen to live where there are no willows or other plants with slender twigs, you can cut and shape your ribs out of any lumber that is suitable for steam bending. I have used oak and ash. Both bend well. If you can't get either of these, experiment with the wood you can get.

According to Bill Tcheripanoff, as interviewed by Joelle Robert-Lamblin, his father used yellow cedar. He soaked the ribs and then cold-bent them, using his teeth to crimp the ribs in the tight bends. I have tried this and it works, but it is very hard on teeth. In general, I don't recommend this technique since you can easily do more damage to your teeth than your whole boat is worth.

Making a Steam Box

A steam box can be any kind of container that will let steam flow over the ribs. You can make the box out of ½-inch (13 mm) or ⅜-inch (10 mm) plywood. You can also make it out of foam insulation board that has a reflective backing. The box should be about 36 inches (91 cm) long with some wires or small dowels going through it for the ribs to rest on while steaming. One end of the box should be open and the other end should be capped. When the ribs are in the box steaming, the open end needs to be covered with a rag to keep the heat in.

Figure 1. *This steam box may look crude but it's actually very effective. The camping stove supplies the heat to generate the steam. The brick on top of the steam box ensures a tight seal. A piece of plywood with a hole in it is used as a lid on the water pot. The hole in the lid matches up with a hole in the bottom of the steam box.*

The source of the steam can be an ordinary cooking pot with about a gallon (4 liter) capacity. The source of heat can be a cook stove if you have one in your shop or a camping stove if you don't. Keep a window open when using a camping stove, to ventilate the fumes. You can also use an electric hot plate if you can find one that throws off enough heat to keep a good flow of steam going.

The steam pot needs a lid with a hole in it. You can either set the steam box right over a hole and have a matching hole in the steam box, or connect the hole in the lid to the hole in the steam box with a hose or a pipe.

Cutting the Rib Stock

As I said, I've used both ash and oak for ribs. If you can get the rib stock from a sawmill before it has been dried, it will bend much more easily than seasoned wood. In either case, cut the wood into strips about 28 inches (71 cm) long and ⅜ inch x ⅜ inch (10 mm x 10 mm) in cross section. Round the edges with a spokeshave to give the ribs a circular cross section. Soak them in water for three or four days. You will need about 40 ribs if you space them 4 inches (10 cm) apart. Allow 10 extra for breakage and wrong bending if you're starting with green wood, and a few more if you're starting with dried wood.

Rib Forms

Figure 2. *You can make an adjustable rib-bending form out of two pieces of plywood.*

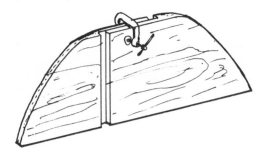

You will need to fix a batten that marks the height of the keelson—just as you would if you were using green twigs. (See Chapter 8 for instructions on rigging that up.) If you want to get more elaborate, you can make an adjustable plywood bending form and bend your ribs over it. This form is most useful for the ribs near the center of the boat. You may need to bend ribs at the ends of the boat freehand or make additional bending forms.

Bending the Ribs

Steam-bending ribs is a little harder than bending green twigs, since you can work them only for about a minute before they cool and stiffen. You can, of course, take a chance and bend the ribs freehand if you can afford to lose a few before you get the shape you want. Unless you have asbestos fingers, you'll need gloves when you remove the ribs from the steam box. When the steam is going strong, you should steam the ribs for 5 to 10 minutes before bending them.

If you can persuade a partner to help you with the rib bending, the process will go a lot easier. After you've bent a rib, you'll need to hold it inside the boat while your partner marks where it meets the gunwales. You will then need to trim the rib ½ inch (13 mm) past the mark, whittle down the ends a little, and slide them into the mortises. As I've pointed out already, you don't need to fit the ribs tightly in the mortises.

As a matter of fact, ribs on traditional boats always seem to have been fitted loosely to give them some room to work as the boat bends in use. If the rib is too tall, trim the ends. If a rib is too short, start over or try to use it on a narrower part of the boat.

If you find that more than a third of your ribs crack or splinter when you are bending them, stop and ponder. You may not have an adequate flow of steam. Turn up the heat under your water pot. If you use a gas stove or camp stove, this should be no problem. Some small electric hot plates simply may not put out enough heat to do the job. If this is the case, try to find a heat source with a higher wattage.

3

APPENDIX

Mortised Deck Beams

Mortised deck beams are shaped like pegged deck beams, but need to be cut longer so they can have tenons on either end. Those tenons must be long enough to go through the gunwales. Although mortised deck beams require more work than the pegged kind, they have a great advantage: They're self-aligning. With pegged deck beams, you need to keep a constant eye on the deck to make sure it doesn't get warped.

Figure 1. With the gunwales spread, mark the position of the deck beams on the gunwales (left). Once you have marked the positions of all the deck beams, you can drill the mortises (right) and square them up with a chisel.

Marking the Mortises

After you've marked the deck beam positions and spread the gunwales, lay a straightedge across both gunwales and draw lines on

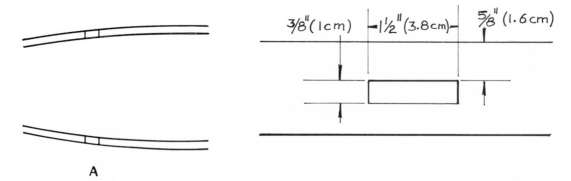

A

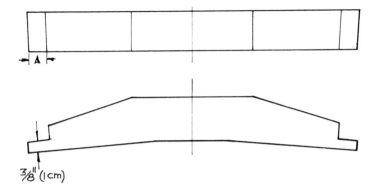

3/8" (1 cm)

Figure 2. Cut tenons on the deck beams to match the mortises. Tenons (A) must be at least as long as the gunwales are thick. You can trim excess after assembly.

either end of where the deck beam will intersect the gunwales. This line will be at an angle to the gunwales and not perpendicular. This is the angle at which you must cut the mortise. Mortises are ⅜ inch (10 mm) tall and 1½ inches (3.8 cm) wide and ⅝ inch (16 mm) from the top edge of the gunwale.

Cutting the Mortises

Drill holes through the gunwales at either end of the mortise and remove the wood in between with a chisel. Remember to drill the holes at an angle to the face but parallel to the top edge of the gunwales.

Cutting the Tenons

Tenons should be cut a little longer than necessary to go through the gunwales and then trimmed after assembly. Mark the tenons as shown in Figure 2. Cut the tenons with a fine-tooth back saw. Clean them up with a chisel. Test their fit in the mortises.

4
APPENDIX

Sails and Rudders

We know for a fact that the Aleuts used both sails and rudders on their kayaks because there are examples of both in museum collections. Strangely, though, I don't know of any photographs or drawings that show either sails or rudders in use. So they must have used them very infrequently—perhaps only to run before the wind. They certainly didn't carry leeboards or any other equipment to make tacking or reaching practical.

I once made a rudder and sail for one of my baidarkas but found them to be more of a nuisance than they're worth. However, if you experiment, you might be able to come up with a combination that will give you some relief from paddling on long trips.

For more background on this topic, read George Dyson's *Baidarka*. You'll also find some innovative sail plans there.

The Rudder

The rudder keeps the boat on course when you are running before the wind. See Figure 1 for construction details. The bottom of the rudder is tied to the drain tube. The top of the rudder has a hollow knuckle, which fits the end of the tailpiece. It is held in place by a line that runs around the cockpit coaming. If you knot the line in the exact center, you can judge your rudder trim by whether the knot is right or left of the cockpit center.

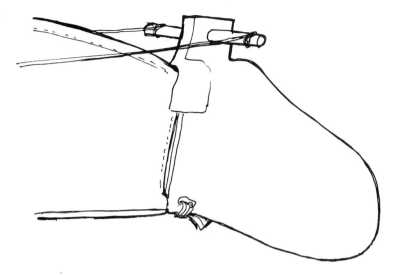

Figure 1. The rudder is tied to the drain tube at the bottom and held in place on top by lines leading to the cockpit.

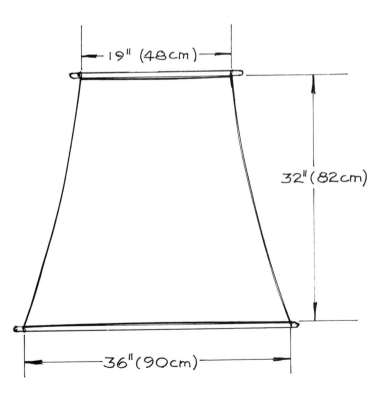

Figure 2. Sample sail plan for a baidarka.

19" (48cm)

32" (82cm)

36" (90cm)

The Sail

The sail plan shown in Figure 2 is based on a drawing by David Zimmerly. To be frank, I found that this amount of sail was ineffective except in fairly high winds. Perhaps this sail area was just right for the strong wind conditions typically encountered by Aleuts.

If you don't live in the Aleutians, you might want to consider increasing the area by 50 percent. The mast is mounted just forward of the second deck beam. To use a sail, you must be sure to install a mast step before you sew on the skin. The mast step is just a block of wood with a hole in it, lashed across two ribs adjacent to the keelson, to accommodate the bottom of the mast.

You will also have to make a hole in the skin of the deck for the mast to slide through. To keep water out of the hole, sew a tube of skin to the hole. This tube will look like a little chimney coming out of the deck. When you don't have a mast in the tube, roll up the tube and tie it off.

Kayak Dimensions and Checklists

APPENDIX

This appendix contains a summary of the boat's dimensions and a number of checklists to give you a quick overview of the boat and the building process.

Boat Dimensions

Figure 1 is a drawing of a completed boat. A summary of some key dimensions appears below. Remember that you may have to adjust some of these dimensions to make the boat fit you or to suit your personal needs and desires.

Total length	16'8" (508cm)
Gunwale length	14'10" (452cm)
Width at front of cockpit (beam)	21" (53cm)
Width at tail end of gunwales	9" (23cm)
Width at bow end of gunwales	7" (18cm)
Inside length of cockpit coaming	24" (61cm)

Inside width of cockpit coaming	18" (46cm)
Depth to sheer at cockpit	8¾" (22cm)
Depth to sheer at bow end of gunwales	6½" (16.5cm)
Depth to sheer at tail end of gunwales	7¾" (20cm)
Total weight	35 lbs (16kg)

Figure 1. Aleut Kayak Frame

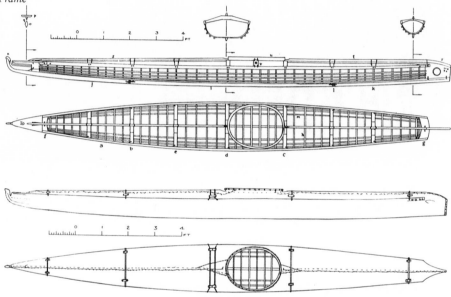

The Parts of the Boat

The following is a list of all the parts that make up your kayak.

2 gunwales

40 ribs

8 hull stringers

7 deck beams

2 bow cross blocks

2 tail cross blocks

1 bow piece

1 tail piece   *(continued)*

3 keel sections

2 deck stringers

1 cockpit coaming

2 coaming stanchions

1 coaming lip (attached to coaming after skin is on)

assorted lashing string

5 deck straps

10 deck strap toggles

1 skin (6 yards of canvas)

oil paint

boiled linseed oil

varnish

Minimum Tool List

The following is the absolute minimum of tools that you need to build the boat according to the instructions in this manual. Traditional builders would have added an adze to this list and deleted the measuring tape.

cross cut saw

carving knife

drill and bit

hammer

measuring tape or yard stick

Advanced Tool List

The following are additional tools that will make the job go a little faster. They are nice to have but not essential.

adze

power saw

hand plane

spoke shave

Shop Requirements

A shop is simply a space that is big enough for you to work on your boat. If the weather is nice, this can even be outside.

space 20' x 8' (6.7m x 3m)

2 saw horses

light

Building Checklist

The following is list of steps in the building of a kayak. This list is meant to help you track your progress. If you dutifully record your progress on this building checklist, then restarting after a break should be as simple as taking up with the next unchecked item on the checklist. If you would like to see where your time went, then you can also record the number of hours spent on each part of the building process.

Buy lumber for a paddle

Make a paddle

If you were able to make a paddle, you're able to build a boat. So proceed.

Buy lumber for your boat

Order canvas

Set up your shop

Set up and level your sawhorses

Cut gunwales

Plane gunwales

Check gunwales for symmetry

Mark gunwales for deck beam positions

Mark gunwales for rib mortises

Drill rib mortises

Spread gunwales with temporary spreaders

Carve deck beams on either side of the cockpit

Install deck beams on either side of the cockpit

Measure elevation of remaining deck beams

Carve and install remaining deck beams

Carve and install bow cross blocks

Carve and install tail cross blocks

Drill and lash deck beams to gunwales

Stain your deck

Turn your deck over and install a temporary keel stringer

Cut or collect your rib stock

Install ribs

Carve the upper bow piece

Install keel sections and upper bow piece

Lash keel sections to the ribs

Cut hull stringers

Shape hull stringers

Lash hull stringers to the ribs

Carve tail piece

Carve deck stringers

Cut cockpit coaming blank

Bend cockpit coaming

Fit deck stringers, cockpit coaming, and tail piece to each other

Lash deck stringers to the deck and the cockpit coaming

Lash cockpit coaming to the gunwales by way of the cockpit stanchions

Install tail piece and lash it to the keelson and back deck stringer

Lash bow deck stringer to the bow piece

Stain all unstained pieces

Oil or varnish the entire hull

Carve toggles for the deck straps

Stretch the skin on the hull

Trim excess canvas

Sew in darts in front and back of the cockpit

Sew the first seam on the skin and install deck straps as you go

Trim along the seam

Sew the second seam

Sew around the cockpit coaming

Cut strip of wood for cockpit lip

Sew cockpit lip around the coaming

Put first coat of paint on the skin

Sand the skin

Put second coat of paint on the skin

Sand the skin

Put final coat of paint on the bottom of the hull

Sand bottom of the hull

Launch your boat

Be careful

Start thinking about your next boat

Glossary

As you build boats and read boatbuilding literature and talk to other boatbuilders, you begin to accumulate new words in your vocabulary. I have collected these words in a glossary and provided some definitions for those who might find some terms foreign.

Baidara—Probably means "boat" in Russian. This is what the Russians called the Aleuts' large boats, which are called umiaks elsewhere in the Arctic.

Baidarka—The Russian word for kayak. The diminutive of baidara.

Chine—Edges in the boat's hull that run fore and aft. In a kayak, a chine is formed by the skin going over one of the hull stringers. Since there are many stringers in a baidarka, chines are soft; that is, there is no abrupt change in angle as the skin passes over them. In contrast, boats such as Greenland kayaks are said to be hard-chined. The term chine is sometimes also used to refer to the hull stringers themselves.

Frame—Another word for rib. In traditional wooden hull boatbuilding, the planking of the hull is nailed through the frames.

Gunwales—These are the two boards that establish the shape of the deck when viewed from above. The gunwales are the main strength members in a kayak and are primarily responsible for stiffening the boat.

Hog—When a boat crests a wave and the ends of the boat sag into the troughs on either side of the crest, this is called hogging. When a boat is built so the keel is higher at the center than at the ends, it is said to be hog bottomed. Baidarkas are not built hog bottomed but they will hog when cresting a wave, especially when loaded.

Keelson—A keel that runs inside the hull of the boat and does not project down below it. In the case of a kayak, the keelson is inside the skin.

Mortise—A hole in a piece of wood into which a tenon is fitted.

Resaw—To resaw a board is to cut it in half with the blade parallel to the faces. If you resaw a ¾ inch x 3 inch board, you get two ⅜ inch x 3 inch boards.

Rip—To rip a board is to cut it down the long dimension, along the grain, rather than across it.

Rocker—The amount of curvature in the keel line, also applied to curvature in the chines. Rocker allows a boat to move between the troughs and crests of heavy seas without undue pitching and plunging, first into the face of a wave and then down into the trough. However, too much rocker in the chines makes for a slower boat on flat water.

Sheer—This is upward curvature in the gunwales from the middle toward the ends. If the gunwales are lower in the middle than at the ends, the boat is said to have some sheer. This is the normal condition in boats. If the gunwales are level from end to end, the boat is said to have no sheer. If the gunwales are higher in the middle than at the ends, the boat is said to have reverse sheer. Do not confuse sheer with rocker, which is the amount of curvature in the keel line.

Stringer—A slender piece of wood running the length of the boat along the hull or deck. Stringers in a kayak support the skin and also give the boat longitudinal stiffness.

Tenon—An extension to a piece of wood that fits into a mortise. A tenon is usually narrower or thinner than the piece of wood it sticks out of.

Umiak—An open skin-on-frame boat. The Aleut version was called a baidara.

References

Here's a list of some books containing information that may be helpful to you when you build your Aleut kayak.

Adney, Edwin T., and Howard I. Chapelle. 1983. *The bark canoes and skin craft of North America*. Washington, D.C.: Smithsonian Institution Press.

    Adney put together the material on canoes, and Chapelle organized the book and added several chapters on skin boats. John Heath provided an appendix on the Eskimo Roll. The book has two drawings of baidarkas. This is a new edition. For a long time, the original edition was the only book that contained any information about traditional craft.

Arima, Eugene Y., Editor. 1991. *Contributions to kayak studies*. Canadian Ethnology Service Mercury Series Paper 122. Hull, Quebec: Canadian Museum of Civilization.

    This book is about kayaks of all kinds, not just baidarkas, but five of the eleven papers are about baidarkas.

Brand, John. 1981. *The little kayak book*. Colchester, Essex, England. Self-published.

    This book reproduces the hull lines of a baidarka in the British Museum. It also has drawings of a number of other kayaks. John Brand followed this book with two more Little Kayak Books, which focus more heavily on Greenland kayaks. John publishes the books himself. His address, should you wish to order from him, is: Bramble

Tye, Stanway Green, Colchester, Essex, CO3 5RA,
Great Britain.

Dyson, George. 1986. *Baidarka*. Edmonds, WA: Alaska
Northwest Publishing Company.

This is the book that first introduced me to baidarkas.
It contains lots of photographs and drawings of genuine
Aleut kayaks. It also contains quite a bit of history of these
craft and has color pictures of the places where Aleuts
paddled these craft. Finally, it has pictures of George
Dyson building all kinds of baidarkas of different sizes
and shapes, continuing, as he puts it, the evolution of
the craft.

Gardner, John. 1987. *The dory book*. Mystic, CT: Mystic
Seaport Museum.

This book has no information about baidarkas but it
does have a good treatment of scarfing short planks to
make long ones. The dory, incidentally, became the
Aleut workboat of choice after the decline of sea otter
hunting and the baidarka.

Robert–Lamblin, Joelle. 1980. "Le kayak Aleoute vu par son
constructeur et utilisateur et la chasse à la loutre de mer."
Objets et Mondes 20 (1): 5 - 20. Paris, France.

This is a fairly thorough overview of Aleut baidarkas
and hunting methods. If you don't read French, or can't
get hold of this article, don't fret; most of the information is available in Dyson's *Baidarka*. The major piece of
new information in this article is baidarka dimensions in
terms of the builder's body dimensions.

Short, Derrel, and Jerry Martini, photographer. "The Kodiak
kayak." *WoodenBoat* magazine #58.

Kodiak kayaks are sufficiently similar to baidarkas for
you to get some good construction hints out of this article.

Zimmerly, David W. 1986. *QAYAQ: Kayaks of Siberia and
Alaska*. Juneau, AK: Division of State Museums, 1986.

This book has two drawings of one-hole baidarkas, one
drawing of a double, and one drawing of a three-holer. It
also has a number of photographs of people in baidarkas.

Zimmerly, David W. 1983. "Building the one-hole Aleut bidarka." *Small Boat Journal*, February/March and April/May 1983.

This construction article appeared in two parts. According to George Dyson, it inspired the building of several dozen baidarkas. Well worth consulting, if you can find a copy of the article.

Index

Wood
  cutting, 42
  drilling, 42–44
  elasticity of, 36–37
  marking of, 41–42
  plugging holes in, 149
  specific gravities of, 36–37
  strength, 36–37
  types of, 34–37

Wood Handbook, 36

Workbench, 33–34

Workmanship, standards of, 41

Work space, 33–34

Z

Zimmerly, David, 158, 169